The Witch-Hunt

F. G. BAILEY

The Witch-Hunt;

or,

The Triumph
of Morality

CORNELL UNIVERSITY PRESS

ITHACA AND LONDON

First published 1994 by Cornell University Press
First printing, Cornell Paperbacks, 1996

Printed in the United States of America

Library of Congress Cataloging-in-Publication Data

Bailey, F. G. (Frederick George)
The witch-hunt; or, The triumph of morality / F. G. Bailey.
p.   cm.
Includes bibliographical references and index.
ISBN 0-8014-3021-6 (cloth : alk. paper)
ISBN 0-8014-8210-0 (paper : alk. paper)
1. Ethnology—India—Bisipara.   2. Witchcraft—India—Bisipara.
3. Caste—India—Bisipara.   4. Bisipara (India)—History.   5. Bisipara
(India)—Social conditions.   6. Bisipara (India)—Religious life and
customs.   I. Title.   II. Title: Triumph of morality.
GN635.14B35   1994
306'.0954'13—dc20   94-3193

Cornell University Press strives to use environmentally responsible suppliers and
materials to the fullest extent possible in the publishing of its books. Such materials
include vegetable-based, low-VOC inks and acid-free papers that are recycled,
totally chlorine-free, or partly composed of nonwood fibers. Books that bear the
logo of the FSC (Forest Stewardship Council) use paper taken from forests that
have been inspected and certified as meeting the highest standards for environ-
mental and social responsibility. For further information, visit our website at
www.cornellpress.cornell.edu.

1   3   5   7   9   Cloth printing   10   8   6   4   2
3   5   7   9   Paperback printing   10   8   6   4

For Mary

Contents

Acknowledgments

For their comments I thank Suzanne Brenner, Susan Love Brown, Roy D'Andrade, Mary K. Gilliland, Paula Levin, Tanya Luhrman, and Erica Prussing.

The Witch-Hunt

Warrior children, a girl and her little brother, returning along a path beside our bungalow from their daily bath in the river. The girl walks behind. She carries on her head the clothing she has washed and a small brass vessel that contained coconut oil.

Introduction

This is a memoir of certain events that took place forty years ago in a village called Bisipara, which lies in the Kondmals, a subdivision of the district of Phulbani in the state of Orissa in eastern India. The people of Bisipara spoke Oriya, the majority language of the state, but in the Kondmals more than half the inhabitants (five in eight) were Konds, who had a different language, Kui. The Konds were indigenous: Bisipara people were intruders who long ago came up from the plains to settle in the Kond hills. They saw themselves, when they looked back on their history, as colonizers and frontiersmen, the representatives of a higher civilization in the land of the barbarian Konds. The Konds saw them mostly as avaricious and unscrupulous interlopers.

The village was named for the Bisois, a collection of about twenty-five households, almost all related by common descent (through males), and a good part of them living along the main street. The Bisois were Hindu by religion and Warrior by caste. As Warriors, they had been the one-time lords of the place, and they still in 1953 tried to think of themselves in that way. About seven hundred people lived in Bisipara then, and a fifth of them were Warriors.

The events—the death of a girl and the troubles that followed—are recorded in my notes, but some scenes, even after forty years, are visually intact in my memory. Some of the thoughts that came

1

to me at the time, but were not written down, still survive; and I have had other thoughts since then. An account of the events, and the accompanying commentary, will, I hope, convey to the reader what it was like to live as a visitor in that place at that time and, with much less assuredness, what it was like to be a native of Bisipara. I was on the outside, looking in. I saw what they did; mostly (after a time) I understood what they said; all the time I struggled to work out what must have been in their minds to make them act and speak that way.

Often it seemed that they had stratagems to immunize themselves against seeing what was really going on, as if they believed they could make the world to their own design by pretending it really was so. Reality, I thought at first, was what I saw and heard, but sometimes I had to change my mind because the reality that I could see did not include all the reality that I sought—the unspoken part of their thoughts and, above all, their motivations. Of one thing, however, I am sure: the community was midway on a journey that would profoundly change it from what it had been. The people of Bisipara knew, more or less, what was happening, and, as individuals, they used that factual knowledge to guide their actions toward their own personal advantage. But, as a community, they defined reality counterfactually, hanging on to the myth that nothing fundamental had changed and no fundamental change was needed. They were not given to institutional reflexivity, to public doubt and public questioning of their moral order, for which their word was *dharma*, the natural order of things. The pattern of society—the morality—that they inherited from the past was still legitimate; new ways were not.

A plain narrative of the events, without commentary and interpretation, is simple enough. A young girl, Susila, took a fever and quickly died. The villagers, finding the death suspicious, held an investigation, identified several culprits, and in the end fastened substantial blame on one of them. It seems that he had been practicing what we would call black magic and had inadvertently caused Susila's death. The inquiry was carried out rather hurriedly—even, some considered, haphazardly—because the villagers wanted the stage clear for the annual celebration of the birthday of the god Sri Ramchandro. Nevertheless, they were eventually able to agree upon the identity of the culprit, and they exacted from him a large fine.

My commentary on these events opens the curtain on a larger and more complicated scene. It portrays a community in the process of change, in which, if one chooses to look at the matter that way, the offender is revealed as a heroic individual who has broken from the chains of the past; he is the dissenter standing up for his rights against an entrenched and conservative establishment. From the opposite point of view he is a troublemaker, a man who rejects the moral order on which society and the good life depend, a man who has trespassed outside the domain where he properly belongs, a man defying his dharma. From a more distant and ethically neutral perspective (mine), the offender's conduct was a threat to those in power, and their determined and successful effort to punish him was made mainly to protect their own privileged position. In doing so, of course, they could say they were protecting the moral order that made their community the good thing they claimed it was.

The story of Susila's death and the forces that it set in motion is also a commentary on the human condition, on certain problems that are universal, on the particular forms that those problems took in that place at that time, and on the solutions that people found—when they could find any. Death, sickness, hunger, infertility (whether of the land, of the livestock, or of women) were seen by people in Bisipara as part of life's equation, the bad things that balance out the good. They knew that taking arms against those troubles would not end them; but they tried. They were not fatalists, as Hindus are sometimes said to be, and as I at first thought they were; later I came to realize that they did not bow to fate without a struggle. At least they wanted explanations. In the end, for those who survived, the problems all came down to making sense of the things that happened: not making them happen or preventing them (although that was certainly welcome when it could be done, which was not often), but simply having an explanation for why things turned out the way they did. In Bisipara, as everywhere, understanding could to some degree neutralize despair.

The explanations that they used invoked divine forces, both good and evil. They also contained the vision of an ideal moral society, which was in many respects very far from the reality in which they lived. Both the divine forces and the moral order were couched in an idiom that, in its specifics, is not familiar to us. But the underlying pattern is certainly familiar. Bisipara's moral order was essentially conservative, even high Tory; it was hierarchical, a framework designed by the divinity, estates ordered by God, comprising high and lowly, each in their place. The offenders were those who disregarded the divine law, resisted the role allotted to them, and so allied themselves, for their own particular selfish benefit, with the forces of evil.

Such explanations, involving mystical forces and the image of a social order that did not exist, were poetic fantasies. But they had objective consequences because people believed them. People did so because the explanations were a comfort; they were, to borrow an idea from Ibsen, "the lies that make life possible."

They had another feature that will become apparent in the story as it unfolds. Tales told in Bisipara to explain why things had gone wrong were also tales that were used to manipulate and control other people.

Stories that explain how the world works are often about making right and wrong choices. In Bisipara, as is the case everywhere except among those who accept the amoral neoclassical economic paradigm, the wrong choice was the self-interested choice. The right choice was one motivated by a concern for the public good. The sophistry of an invisible hand, which causes selfish actions by selfish people to be for the good of us all, was unknown in Bisipara and would have seemed patently untrue. Their world worked in precisely the opposite way. There was an invisible hand in their philosophy, and it was moved to action by choices that were selfishly made, but it reacted to the *wrongness* of those choices, and its actions were not, in the short run, beneficial; they were harmful. Moreover it acted indirectly. It brought down sickness and misfortune not immediately on the offender but indiscriminately, on anyone at all, so that righteous people then felt compelled to search out the wrongdoers and make them mend their ways.

Much of Bisipara's array of wrongdoing is familiar to us. The people had strong ideas about property and about theft. They recognized the responsibilities of public office and kept a keen eye open for embezzlement. They were pessimists in that respect, believing that very few people would resist the temptation to cheat or to steal, if they thought they could get away with it. They were especially sensitive about freeloading, and, when there was communal work to be done, they kept careful tally of who turned up and who did not. They were convinced that no normal person, whatever sanctimonious claims he or she might make, would voluntarily put public welfare ahead of private gain.

They had standards of good behavior and of the good society that in many ways resemble ours. They abhorred incest; they disapproved of fornication; and in public they were embarrassed by smut. They detested various modes of feeling or action that we would count as inhumane; they were aware of compassion; they felt responsibility for each others' welfare; they valued trust (but were nervous about trusting each other); and they had a great deal to say about duty and mutual obligation.

But, as the tale will show, they were also swift to condemn actions that we sometimes praise. Bisipara people did not admire entrepreneurs. They were suspicious of the market and knew nothing of its purported socially beneficial effects. They detested innovation and the things that entrepreneurs do, because entrepreneurs, in the process of benefiting themselves, create equivalences that did not exist before; they blur the lines that once clearly separated one category from another. They make things uncertain. Bisipara people did not like to see men or women shape their own lives, if the shaping departed in any respect from convention. Rugged individualism was not something to brag about. Public opinion in Bisipara, within the limits of its power (which was indeed limited), penalized such people.

Of course thrusting and ambitious persons existed there, as they do everywhere; people, some more than others, did look to their own advantage even if they had to defy conventions to do so. In Bisipara, as among us, there was an inescapable tension between duty and expediency, between doing what is right and winning out. The line that marked the boundary between individual autonomy and the domain where the collectivity ruled was frequently contested, and what others called duty to the community often presented itself to the individual as a mere cover for exploitation by the community. Conversely, the same individuals, feathering their own nests, would claim to be acting for the common good.

The ultimate falsity of this situation was that those who took the lead in protecting the traditional structure and traditional values of their community—those who used the language of the moral order to put upstarts back in their places—seemed often to be motivated more by their own self-interest than by a concern for tradition and the public good. Public opinion was at best an indirect protector of ancestral values because the public was composed of self-interested people, shining examples of "economic man," who mostly were ready to violate custom and propriety whenever they saw a personal advantage in doing so. The situation also had its irony, because the consequence of what they did often was in fact to preserve the traditional order, or at least its facade.

Warrior street was a two-hundred-yard stretch of earth, a little wider than a tennis court, running from east to west. Men, children, and dogs hung around in the street; women never loitered there. In the center of the street, between the two rows of houses, was the village meeting house, the *mandap,* and, farther to the east, a pergola-like construction of stout poles and horizontal beams that provided a shade under which men could sit and take

Warrior street looking eastward. The central building is the mandap, or meeting house (rear view). The house on the left is that of Jodu, the postmaster. In the right foreground is the house of the three Herdsman brothers and next to it Tuta's house. The substantial house farther down the row is the sirdar's. The smiling man is Sudersun, the youngest of the sirdar's half-brothers.

their ease. On the northern side, a little to the west of the mandap and inserted in the row of houses, was a temple dedicated to Sri Ramchandro, a manifestation of the Hindu god Vishnu. Like all streets in Bisipara, although grander than the others, Warrior street was a public space surrounded by houses, a dirt-surfaced equivalent of a village square, a thoroughfare only for pedestrian traffic. Access to the street was by narrow footpaths. (No one in Bisipara owned a motor vehicle at that time, except me). In the summer the street's surface was a carpet of dust; in the wet season it was muddy and slippery, sprouting weeds and grass.

A poor man's house was a single room, with a door facing away from the street and a path leading round the side and giving onto a yard and a fenced garden. Houses were private places; all

A simple and inexpensive way to build the wall of a house.

of them, rich or poor, presented a blank wall to the street, no
windows and no door. Better-off families had a cluster of buildings sited around a courtyard: a main room where the husband
and wife and their small children slept, and where the grain was
stored in huge baskets sealed inside and out with a plaster of
earth and cow dung; one or two other rooms where older children or a widowed parent or visitors might sleep; and a cowshed.
A few compounds housed two or more families (always related
through their male heads) living around a courtyard. A single
passageway, gated to keep out straying cattle and goats, led to the
street. In the more substantial households this passageway was
roofed, so that one entered the courtyard as through a tunnel.

A house was built around a wooden frame. Older houses,
constructed by wealthy men, had solid wooden doors, ornately
carved, and walls of wooden planks, set vertically or horizontally
and plastered over with the brownish-yellow mixture of earth
and cow-dung. A simpler and cheaper method was to make the

The carved pillar supports a roof over the veranda of a rich man's house (the sirdar's).

Replastering a wall in the merchant's shop in Warrior street. Galvanized steel buckets were rare; the only other ones in Bisipara belonged to our bungalow. The woman on the right is Rua the widow.

walls from a wattle of saplings, stuck vertically in the earth foundation and daubed with straw-reinforced mud. Doors for such houses were flimsy, woven from split bamboo. Most roofs were thatch. The poor used rice straw, which had to be renewed or at least repaired every year; those who could afford it hired people to collect a tough grass that grew in the forest and was good for three or four years. House walls, the earth on which they stood, and the thatched roofs were monochrome, each a slight variation on the same khaki color.

The better houses had a double roof to insulate them from the heat, the lower part flat and made of earth, tented above with thatch. This arrangement was expensive in labor and materials but had the extra benefit of shielding the interior of the room from the many objectionable creatures and insects that infest a thatch roof. It also provided some protection from fires, which were not infrequent; with luck, the thatch would burn and the house be left intact. The drawback was that smoke from the cooking hearth had nowhere to escape except through a small barred opening set high in the inner wall or through the doorway; smoke filters, albeit very slowly, through thatch. All but the poorest households had a cowshed or at least an open-sided shelter to protect the cattle and goats from sun and rain. Behind the courtyards stretched long gardens, where the people planted maize and grew beans, brinjals, "foreign" brinjals (*bilati baigono:* their name for tomatoes), cucumbers, courgettes, pumpkins, and the unappealing slimy okra. A five-foot wattle fence protected the crops and gave the garden and the courtyard a measure of privacy.

At the western end of the street of the Warriors there was a shop with a rusted corrugated-iron roof showing through a thin layer of badly maintained thatch. It sold cloth (cheap, subsidized stuff, which the villagers sometimes bought but did not much like), tea, sugar, rice, powdered milk, molasses, various cooking oils, coconut oil (which women used on their hair), soap, matches, kerosene, and a few other everyday things. Many customers made their purchases not with cash but with paddy (rice in the husk), which the shopkeeper added to the stock that he sold to other customers. (Cash was scarce, and no one habitually carried it around.) Mostly the shop's business was in trading for turmeric from villages farther into the hills. Bisipara people, as customers, preferred to patronize the Wednesday market in the district headquarters, despite the two-hour walk each way.

At the other end of the street a well-to-do Christian family owned a *pakka* house, one made of bricks and mortar, plastered over and whitewashed. (*Pakka* is a word applied to anything refined, well finished, or perfected. It is opposed to *kacha*, things that are rough, makeshift, or coarse.) The house had a flat roof, accessible by an outside stairway. The roof was a safe place to dry grains and produce and a cool place to sleep in the hot weather. Of the 179 households in Bisipara, only two, one rich and the other poor, each with two individuals, a widowed mother and an adult son, were Christian. All the rest were Hindu.

There were two other streets fifty yards to the north of Warrior street and running parallel to it: one where Distillers lived (*Sundisai*) and another for Potters (*Kumbharsai*). They were less grand than Warrior street, and neither contained any public building. A short distance to the west of this cluster was a mixed-up area that housed people of several castes. There were a few small shops, some houses where Weavers lived and worked, and a temple. This area was called *Hatopodera*, which means "marketplace." Two hundred yards off to the north and east was a long, narrow, dogleg, slightly slumlike street (*Panosai*) that housed untouchables of a caste called Pano. Each street had its own well.

A grandson of the well-to-do Christian family (he lived in another place where his job as a government official took him) had a university degree, the only person from the village at that time to have scaled those heights. Indeed, only two boys (and no girls) had attended the high school in the district headquarters, and both were plucked in matriculation, the final examination. (*Plucked* is a nineteenth-century Anglo-Indian word, adopted into Bisipara's vernacular. It means to fail an examination. The term may be used with pride by those who fail; at least they have done the course. An apocryphal brass plate, said to be seen in cities, boasts: "Bachelor of Laws, Plucked.") The village had an upper primary school, but most people were not much schooled. Some were farmers, owning land, others worked as day laborers, and many went in for petty trading. A few, who counted themselves successful, had minor jobs in government: a policeman, one or two office peons, and several schoolmasters.

The villagers saw marked differences in wealth among themselves. A few had possessions that were conspicuously expensive. Four households owned breach-loading shotguns; those four, plus one other, had bicycles, ponderous one-speed large-framed machines with reinforced double front forks. Two-thirds of the households in Bisipara owned some land, the main source of wealth, but the distribution was very uneven. Some households had many fields; others had nothing more than the vegetable garden behind the house. About a fifth of the households were rich enough to lend paddy to neighbors who ran short in the autumn before the first harvests ripened. (The loans were a matter of business, interest being charged at 100 percent if the paddy was from the last harvest, when it counted as seed paddy, and 50 percent if older. Some people prospered from lending paddy.) Youths from poor families (and a few married men) hired themselves out as laborers for the growing season, June to January, receiving food and clothing and a modest sum of money from their masters. About twenty people supported themselves that way in 1953. A few were employed year-round, including three women and four men working for the shopkeeper-trader.

These differences in wealth, clear and important for the villagers, were not at first apparent to an outsider. The standard of living seemed uniformly low. Everyone went barefoot; everyone wore thin cotton clothing, and their dress styles did not much vary. They all caught malaria. They all endured attacks of dysentery. They defecated in the fields or along the river bank, and no house had a privy (except the pakka Christian house, which hired an old woman of the Sweeper caste to come each morning and take away the night soil). Everyone ate rice (*bhato*), lentils (*dali*), and spiced vegetables (*torkari*); everyone had one main meal at noon and two snacks, morning and evening. (In the hot season the main meal was eaten after dusk.) The better-off drank tea with the morning snack; the poor drank the water in which yesterday's rice had been boiled. The wealthy did not go hungry in the weeks before the new harvest came in; the poor usually did.

There was no electricity, no piped water, no sewage system, and no telephone. No one read newspapers. In 1953, places like Bisipara were untouched by the revolution of cheap gadgetry. There were no transistor radios; individuals could not shut themselves off from those around them by entering the vast impersonal world of ready-made entertainment. There were no cassette players. There were not even flashlights. A safety razor was a novelty that a few men kept. There were no ballpoint pens and no fountain pens that functioned. (On festive occasions a fountain pen was sometimes displayed in the top pocket of a man's shirt.) Those few who could write and the fewer still who had occasion to write used scratch pens and a bottle of ink or a pencil. In school, the children made their letters on slates.

There was nothing in the village made of plastic. Water pots and cooking pots were clay or brass. Pans, bowls, platters, and containers were mostly brass, very heavy, and scoured each day with sand and wood-ash to make them bright and shining; there were some aluminum utensils; most houses had a large iron cauldron, used for boiling paddy before husking it; and every house had a two-handled, bowl-shaped iron frying pan. A few could boast one or two robust half-pint glass tumblers; none had glazed crockery. The newspapers that came to us from Calcutta and from Liverpool were eagerly salvaged and pasted as decorations over the beautifully carved wooden pillars of the meeting house. Our four-ounce tins of baby food, emptied, achieved the status of near-currency. Women and little girls, who walked through our garden on their way to bathe in the river, abandoned the small elegantly shaped brass vessels in which they carried coconut oil to anoint their long hair and proudly balanced on their heads, instead, Heinz galvanized tins, which, having been cleaned with ash and sand, soon rusted. Bisipara's material culture was poor enough (or perhaps efficient enough) to generate virtually no trash.

The nearest medical services, which no one trusted, were eight miles away in the district headquarters, Phulbani, where about two thousand people lived. The nearest large town was Berhampur (population 60,000), ninety-eight miles distant along a road that, for all but the last twenty miles at the Berhampur end, was not paved. I knew of only a dozen people in Bisipara who had been as far as Berhampur (on their way as pilgrims to Bhubaneswar and Puri).

A quarter of a mile north of the old village was New street (*Nuasai*), where the houses stood apart from one another and had gardens on three sides. The earliest houses there had been built only a generation before. Houses in the old streets of Bisipara were crowded together, wall to wall, with their long narrow gardens extending behind them. In the old days, before British administration expanded into the upland areas (the incursion began in the 1830s), each street was protected by an eight-foot fence of stakes driven into the ground, running round the backs of the gardens, and closed at each end by a gate. It protected the village against enemies and against the animals of the forest. The Kond hills were then a great wilderness, thinly populated. A soldier campaigning in the hills about 1840, when the region was still unpacified, estimated sixteen people to the square mile. Even as late as 1951 the density was only 100 to the square mile, and only on market day in Phulbani, in the market itself, did one get a very slight reminder of the multitudes who mark the Indian urban scene, people shoulder-to-shoulder extending from here to infinity.

Communities in the Kond hills were small parcels, distinct, and widely spaced from one another. Bisipara still in 1953 gave the impression of being walled in and gated, although the fortifications had long since rotted away, and all of the people alive then depended for their continued existence, at least in part, on links beyond Bisipara. But much of their life was lived inwardly, focused on each other. They had no media window on the world's diversity, nothing much to distract them from the unwavering inward scrutiny. About a quarter of the population—almost all the married women—had been born in other villages, but, my wife and myself apart, no one lived there who was a stranger to the close horizons, the total intrusiveness, and the diminished individuality that characterize life in small communities.

Everyone in Bisipara worked, most of them at hard physical tasks. Many people had chronic problems with malaria and with various forms of dysentery. Small children died, especially in the winter months between October and January. My genealogies include that of a woman with ten children, none of whom survived the second year of life. She held the record, but there were many other genealogies that showed only two or three survivors from many children born.

The reader should know that a capital initial letter indicates the name of a caste; the same word, without the capital, refers to an occupation. Thus a Potter is a person of the Potter caste, and a potter is a person who makes pots. (All potters were Potters, just as all barbers were Barbers, and all washermen were Washermen. But not all Potters were potters, or Barbers barbers, or Washermen washermen; some made a living other ways. Conversely not all weavers were Weavers and no Warriors were warriors.)

Oriya and Kui words are italicized at first appearance, excepting those (like panchayat or sirdar or raja or rupee or anna) that appear in English dictionaries. A glossary is provided.

The "ethnographic present," generally used from this point onward to describe buildings, landscapes, customs, customary beliefs, and sometimes states of mind, refers to the 1950s and does not imply that Bisipara is now as it was then. In some respects it may be; in others not. I do not know.

1

Susila's Death

The hot weather in Bisipara makes itself felt early in February and continues, increasingly oppressive, until the middle of June, when the monsoon rains break. People do not exert themselves if they can avoid it. The two or three weeks before the rains come are insufferably humid, day and night. Various things that live outside sense the change and seek shelter indoors, in dark corners or in the roof or under the big baskets in which grain is stored. These include the krait, a placid but very poisonous snake of the cobra family. Over a period of three weeks in 1953 five kraits were caught and killed in the bungalow in which we lived.

Bisipara is almost two thousand feet above sea level, and the highest shade temperature I recorded in 1953 was 106°F, by no means unbearable by the standards of the north Indian plains, but hot enough to make the local people complain. The ground itself gets so hot that they, who go year-round barefoot over rough jungle pathways, moving always with the grace of dancers, flip-flop awkwardly around the village in tattered sandals. During the day they try to stay indoors, behind thick walls and a closed door, following the Indian custom of shutting out the heat. The main meal is eaten after dusk, and night is the time for activity.

They prefer to travel at night, if the journey is long and they plan to stay over. They walk (barefoot because the ground has

cooled) in parties or at least in pairs, with a storm lantern, shouting now and again to frighten away wild animals, mostly bears,
which attack if surprised but clear off if they have warning. The
noise also helps, I was told by a young man, to scare off *bhutos*,
the ghosts of persons who died in unfortunate circumstances—
suicides, for instance, or women in childbirth. Although in most
respects perfectly human in form, a bhuto can be identified, because it is outsize and because its feet point backward. Bhutos
hang around the outskirts of villages, outside the community's
boundary, under the eerie aerial-rooted banyan trees or near out-
lying and alien buildings (such as our three-room brick-and-tile
bungalow, which had been built by the government for the convenience of officials on tours of inspection). So, to scare away
bhutos and (more likely) to make an impressive arrival, a party
of travelers, reaching their destination, beat drums and light a
pressure lantern (always called "Petromax" whatever the make).
Traveling at this time of the year was rarely done for casual visiting, but usually to attend a festival (*jatra*) or, most frequent,
to take part in wedding festivities. March and April were the
marrying months. By then all the harvests (grains and pulses and
vegetables) were gathered, and the year's cultivation had ended.

The end of March and the first week in April sees the high point
of Bisipara's festive year, what elsewhere in northern India is
called the *Ram Lila* (the sport of Ram, *amorous* sport, according to
my Oriya dictionary) and in Bisipara is called *Ramnobomi* (Ram's
birthday). It is a two-week recitation by village men of the twenty-
four thousand couplets of the epic *Ramayana* (day and night,
every night and well into the night, the reciters taking turns)
combined with the enactment of key episodes mixed in with far-
cical performances ridiculing authority. On the final day they put
on a gigantic spectacle at which the demon King Ravana's palace
(a mock-up made of straw) is burned. In 1953 this last occasion
was attended by hundreds of people, who came, on foot and
at night, from the villages around, some as far as twenty miles
away. Order was kept by two young policemen, a plainclothes
detective from the Criminal Investigation Department and a uni-

formed subinspector, who walked their beat together, hand in hand. My notes show that the village fund (raised by a house-by-house subscription, supplementing other income from fields donated to Sri Ramchandro's temple and from fines exacted by the village council, the panchayat) made the policemen a present of two rupees "to buy themselves refreshments." In 1953 this festival took place between March 23 and April 6.

On March 18, a Wednesday, about nine o'clock in the morning when I was sitting in a shuttered room in the bungalow typing up notes, a man who worked for me, Romeschandro Mahakhudo, a Herdsman by caste, entered the room quite abruptly, in a state of obvious excitement—or perhaps alarm—and said I should go with him at once. The reason he gave was that a *devata*, which I knew to be a divinity, demon, or spirit, was "fastened on." I had been there just over six months, and Romesh (that transliteration comes nearest in English to how the villagers pronounced his name) knew the limits of my comprehension of Oriya and normally took pains to speak clearly and distinctly; but not this time. I had not much idea what he was talking about, but the body language of urgency was clear enough, and I grabbed a notebook and camera and went along with him. The camera was inappropriate, so much so that even now, after many years, I feel embarrassed.

He took me to a courtyard in Warrior street. My memory is of seeing several men standing around or sitting on the narrow verandas built against the outside walls of the rooms and notic-ing that they did not belong to that household. Romesh led me into one of the rooms, and there I saw a sight that I have not for-gotten. At first, coming in from the sunlight, I found it difficult to see anything because the only light came from the doorway and from a small barred opening high in the wall facing into the courtyard, a window without glass. The room, a rectangle about ten by fifteen feet, was filled with smoke from a charcoal fire burning in a flat iron dish in the center of the floor. The smoke was aromatic because a man squatting near it (a man from the Potter caste, who had a name as a *gunia*, a diviner) was feeding the fire with green leaves from a lime tree (the citrus variety, not the linden). Lime smoke is reckoned a purifier. Over the pan of coals was a charpoy, which is a bed about five feet long and eighteen inches high, strung like a hammock. On the bed lay a girl I knew, Susila, about sixteen years old. Her father, Syamo Bisoi, a quiet man in early middle age, was respected as a *baidyo*, a doctor proficient in herbal medicines. My genealogies show that Susila had a younger brother and sister, but I cannot recall them now, as I still recall Susila. She had come to the bungalow, several weeks earlier, with a festering cut, which was healed quite quickly by a saline solution. (None of the villagers believed that salt and water worked; they thought I was holding out on some more exotic ingredient.) Susila was strikingly beautiful, with the demeanor of many adolescent girls in that place, somehow combining modesty with flirtatiousness.

Now she lay on the bed, naked except for a thin silver waistbelt and the richly colored woven cloth that women pass between their legs, the ends tucked into the belt. When I entered the room, her mother, who was squatting near her head, spread a small cotton towel over her daughter's breasts. Her father stood at the foot of the bed. There were several women in the room, but their faces have not stayed with me. There was a Warrior man from the neighboring courtyard, a household distantly related to Syamo; this man was a skilled carpenter and had a reputation for having good sense and giving sound advice. People sought him out when they had real trouble.

Shortly after I arrived, another Potter came and stood just inside the door. I knew him too; he was a *maitro* (friend) of Susila's father. With a maitro one has a special kind of friendship, notionally absolute and uncalculating; the person helps unconditionally. These alliances are ritually sealed, sometimes arranged by parents when boys are still small, at other times struck in adolescence by the boys themselves. Often the accident of bearing the same given name is reason enough to make the covenant. Such friendships should last a lifetime and are marked by especially generous help when there is a marriage or a death or any of the lesser crises that punctuate a normal life. Maitro friendship can be covenanted, too, between girls, but tends not to last unless, by chance, they go in marriage to the same village. There is one significant condition; the maitro must belong to a different caste. It is as if we were to have customary covenanted friendships that had to be between Jew and Catholic, black and Hispanic, Anglo and Asian, and so on. Because people marry only within their own caste, it follows that a maitro friend is never a relative. In time of real adversity, people said, a maitro is the better help; kinfolk can be fractious.

I did not stay there long. The smoke made it hard to breathe, and I recall a first thought (about which I fortunately did nothing) that this was no atmosphere for someone so obviously sick; there were too many people present. Susila should have been in a clean bed in a clean white empty room, like a private ward in a hospital. But this room was crowded and dark, anything but clean and sterile; the floor, warm and smooth and pleasant against my bare feet, I knew was made of mud and cow dung. These thoughts were momentary. I had been in Bisipara long enough to know that their culture was not mine, and this was a sickroom, Bisipara-style, with most people there not to provide medical services but to show sympathy and support: the more people the more support. Treatment for sickness in Bisipara is as much a social as a clinical matter. On this occasion the support was given in silence; no one spoke. The women were not wailing, as they do at a funeral or when they hear of a death. I have seen them turn that performance on and off; on one occasion I photographed the switch, the camera transforming a tear-stained face into a beaming smile. But in Susila's room, it seemed to me, the quiet emotions were not in the least contrived. The room was sharp with a total transfixing anxiety.

Then the girl started into a fit, her head thrown back, showing the whites of her eyes. Her father held on to her feet and someone, I think a woman, came forward and leaned across the girl, pinning down her arms to stop her throwing herself off the bed. I do remember her mother snatching the cloth from the girl's body and vainly trying to stuff it between her grinding teeth. Around Susila's neck was a cord of thick black cotton threaded onto a small brass case (the size and shape of a spent twenty-two cartridge). The thread was sacred, acquired through a ritual (called *brata*) performed each August to honor Lakshmi. It served as an amulet, a bringer of luck and a shield against misfortune. At the time I did not know of its significance. A vein in her neck was swelling against the cord, and I said for them to cut the cord. One of the Potter men murmured something, probably a protest, but the carpenter went out and came back with a knife and cut the cord. They were often quite pragmatic about their divinities; those that failed to deliver were put aside. Just after the cord was cut, Susila's fit subsided, I suppose by chance.

Romesh went back to the bungalow and returned with the small metal box in which I kept medicines. Susila had a fever, and I intended to give her what we took daily as a prophylactic against malaria. It was called Paludrine. It was very effective, not only as a preventive but also as a cure, if administered soon enough. But on this occasion it did not get administered at all. I handed her father the appropriate dose—they were tablets—and he tried to put one in her mouth. But she kept her jaw tightly locked, and when we eventually thought to powder up the tablets in water, she would not or could not swallow, and most of the water dribbled down her chin.

I went outside and had a short conference with several of the men: the sirdar (who was headman of the village and its hinterland, and the senior man in the Bisoi lineage), the carpenter who had cut the cord, Susila's father, one of the Potters, and Romesh. It was a conference with little discussion. The carpenter said, several times and vehemently, that this was not a devata, it was sickness. (As you will learn, for most people in Bisipara those two things were not incompatible.) The sirdar kept a poker face, as he usually did, saying nothing. No one contradicted the carpenter, but when I said I could take her to the hospital in Phulbani in my Austin van (now it would be called a truck) and would do so immediately, they looked doubtful, and eventually the sirdar, evidently accustomed to putting a collective feeling into words, said they would talk it over and come to tell me.

So I picked up the camera and walked the hundred yards back to the bungalow, reflecting that if I had the skill and the equipment I might have been able to inject an antimalarial drug into her. (I know now, but did not then, that some medications can be delivered into the rectum of a patient who cannot swallow. What Bisipara's interpretation of my doing that would have been, I find hard to imagine.) In the two years I lived in the village I several times speculated, when a calamity struck, about what I might have done to avert it. That morning I did not dwell on the idea and went back to my typing. I had been away from the bungalow not much more than half an hour.

They were accustomed to death in Bisipara. People seemed to grieve, particularly, as is everywhere the case, for those close to them. They expected the very old to die, as we do. They expected infants to die, an attitude that made me uneasy. (It would not have seemed strange to my own grandparents. My paternal grandmother had, I think, five children die in infancy; five survived.) But I sensed that there was something especially wrong in the case of Susila. This feeling began at the outset with Romesh and his untypically agitated behavior, and it was strengthened by the way people conducted themselves later (I will come to that); it was suggested again by the quiet but palpable distress of the people, men and women, in the sickroom. Inasmuch as I thought of it at the time, I probably concluded that they felt as I felt: that it was wrong that someone young and beautiful and full of life should be taken before all those old ones, who surely had no joy left in living anyway (I too was young, forty years ago). Bisipara people did indeed have that sense; youth was not the time to die. But it turned out that more was involved in this untimeliness than I had thought.

Susila, I was to learn later the same day, had cerebral malaria. The first convulsion had come the previous evening, and she had been ill through the night. Cerebral malaria is endemic in that upland region. Malaria they had all over Orissa, and at that time the authorities were just beginning an intensive effort to control it with pesticidal sprays. But the malaria in the region where Bisipara was situated included a strain of a special kind, less often found in the coastal region. Orissa has a coastal plain, averaging about forty miles wide and containing four of the state's thirteen districts and just under half its total population, which then was fourteen and a half million. The hills, rising to the west, are divided between the remaining nine districts, one being Phulbani, a subdivision of which is the Kondmals, where Bisipara lies. The British, acquiring the coastal regions in the eighteenth century, knew nothing of the hill areas until the 1830s when they went up there in pursuit of a tributary princeling, the Raja of Gumsur, who had bolted into the hills after defaulting on his taxes and defying the tax collector. There they discovered a tribe, the Konds, who not only practiced female infanticide but also perpetrated a spectacular form of human sacrifice called *meriah*. There follows a long tale of imperial bungling, preceded by a pained weighing, in a series of memoranda, of moral duty (to suppress human sacrifice) against the cost of taking over a region that clearly would not yield much revenue.

The Meriah Wars lasted about twenty years before the region was entirely subjugated and its inhabitants rendered more or less docile. The reason for this long campaign was not the military skills of the people who lived in the Kond hills (they had bows and arrows and battle axes), but the presence of the anopheles mosquito and the species *falaparum* of the parasitic protozoan genus *Plasmodium*, which causes cerebral malaria. Each winter an expedition went into the hills, and each winter a high proportion of the soldiers, who were Oriyas coming from the plains, and, I suspect, a still higher proportion of their British officers, died of malaria. In 1953 there was—perhaps still is—a European graveyard in Russelkonda (now Bhanjanagar), where the road begins the climb from the plains into the hills. In the dozen or so graves that still had headstones, all ranks from colonel down to ensign were memorialized; all had died of fever.

Cerebral malaria was thus a great protector for the hill people, at least for those who themselves survived the disease. By World War II drugs had been invented that were successful in preventing or curing the symptoms of malaria, including cerebral malaria, if dealt with in time—first mepacrine (quinacrine), which yellowed the skin, giving the taker a jaundiced look, then Paludrine, then more sophisticated long-lasting things. Villagers had no easy access to Paludrine, the drug we used in 1953, but few adults died of cerebral malaria. Small children did. Malaria was endemic. For most adults an attack was like a bad dose of flu, something not unexpected, especially in the winter. A few unlucky ones eventually had their livers destroyed, the result of repeated bouts of malaria, and died very unpleasantly. But the kind of malaria that led to convulsions and a quick death rarely visited after infancy. Susila, evidently, was an exception.

There was another feature that did not fit the pattern. Malaria is carried by the anopheles mosquito. Mosquitoes breed in still water and they have a limited flying range. Water lies everywhere in the monsoon season (mid-June to early September), when Bisipara gets between fifty and sixty inches of rain. But the rain comes down fast and the water turns over rapidly enough to limit the mosquitoes' breeding chances. People reckon this a time of sickness, all the more distressing because there is much work to do planting paddy seedlings. They suffer from chills and aches, for they work even in the rain, men and women, bent double under the partial shelter of a rain hat (a yard in diameter, made of bamboo and leaves), ankle deep in the mud of a paddy field, planting thousands of seedlings, one by one. Their backs hurt and they get colds and complain of stiff joints and aching muscles, but attacks of malaria are not common at that time.

From September until early January the torrential rains are replaced by occasional showers. Water is everywhere. The irrigated paddy fields, which lie around the village, are under two or three inches of still water. Pools and ponds, and even the leaf cups, which people use to hold their food and discard after use, are replenished by the showers and make ideal places for mosquitoes to breed. So winter is the time when mosquitoes are about, and

Planting a large stream-irrigated field with paddy seedlings. The field belongs to the merchant-shopkeeper, a Distiller.

winter is the time when attacks of fever come, and it is the time when small children die.

By January, surface water is drying out, and it has gone altogether by early April. Even the big eighty-yard-wide river that flows beside Bisipara, the Salki, shrinks to pools and damp sand. There are no longer so many places for mosquitoes to breed, and attacks of malaria become less common. But Susila was laid low after the middle of March. On that score too her illness was exceptional, something that normally should not have happened.

In the afternoon about two o'clock, when people usually sleep at that time of the year, a delegation came to the bungalow and asked me to drive Susila to Phulbani to the government hospital. The delegation had more clout than I would have anticipated if I had thought about it at the time. Nor would I have predicted its composition. I did not think much then, because I was impatient, feeling that they had already wasted some hours that probably mattered. The girl's father was there, and the carpenter, and Romesh (who had gone home for his afternoon sleep), several other men whose faces I do not recall, and the sirdar along with another Bisoi, Jodu, who was the village postmaster, a prosperous man who owned many fields and was the fortunate father of four sons and only two daughters.

The surprise for me lay in the joint presence of the sirdar and Jodu, for each one led a faction in the group of Bisipara Warriors. (A faction is *dolo*, or sometimes they use the English word *party*.) The two were descendants (through males) of a common ancestor, but so far back that no one could fill out the genealogy. (Genealogies get rewritten to fit present-day enmities and alliances, so that, I suspect, this ignorance of past linkages may have been a strategic convenience.) Jodu and the sirdar were more or less instant and automatic opponents, the one supporting whatever the other opposed. They argued in meetings of the village panchayat (the sirdar usually had one or another henchman to do his speaking for him); if they did talk directly to one another it was invariably with the elaborate politeness of controlled antipathy.

The rivalry between the parties was ritualized. Funerals or weddings in the other faction called for mourning or shared rejoicing and for contributions (usually of food for the expensive feasts that such occasions demanded), but to a lesser degree than similar occasions in one's own faction. The lines of cleavage usually followed the lines of known descent, but not always; sometimes brothers quarreled or a father and son fell out, and then one of them might underline the distancing by going over to the other faction. This behavior was felt to be extreme, but I knew of two instances at that time, one in Syamo's own compound. I cannot find any account of the origins of the dolo split in my notes, and all that remains is a memory that it had to do with the present sirdar's grandfather or great-grandfather usurping the office from an ancestor of the other party. It sounds plausible; a lot of my notes about Bisipara read like raw material for a political soap opera.

On this occasion, however, the two men stood side by side. Jodu spoke, making the formal request, and all that I needed to do was remind them of the van's size and how many people it could carry. Reflecting later, my first thought about the presence of the two rivals was that this had something to do with me; that perhaps they had imagined I might be reluctant and thought their joint presence would lend extra pressure and make clear to me that this was something that all the village considered important. But the idea and the suggestion had come from me in the first place, so that made no sense, unless there had been some monumental miscommunication. Reflecting further, I decided that the message was not for me; their joint action was a message to themselves and to the community. Susila's sickness evidently was a serious matter, a catastrophe, more important than faction rivalry (*doladoli*), and a concern to them all, whatever their faction.

I did not think about it at the time, but later, remembering that four hours had gone by while they made up their minds, I realized that the decision to take Susila to the government hospital must not have been easy for them. I do not know who argued which way, but I think I can plausibly reconstruct what must have been in their minds. At that time I still thought, unreservedly, that for people who are seriously ill a hospital is the right place to be. I still think so, but with reservations coming from later experiences. The natural thought (for me) is that hospitals are places where people go to be cured. It is painful to be told, in a particular case, that there will be no cure. In a curious and thoroughly unreasoning way, dying in our culture is not easily accepted as a natural event; one looks around to find someone to blame, for a reason to be angry. I recall with distaste a hospital in Liverpool—I had not heard of hospices in those days—where the terminally ill were sent, and where, it was rumored, the doctors were long over the hill and the nurses, mostly male, robbed the dead of their rings. The institution, I thought, was not worthy to be called a hospital. What I did not realize, until after that day in 1953, was that in the eyes of the people of Bisipara the government hospital in Phulbani was a place to die. But at the same time people also knew that there alone, if one could influence the right people, it might be possible to receive the modern medicines that could work a seemingly miraculous cure. The generic term for this miraculous cure was *injection*, known in the village by that same English word.

Knowing this, I know now why they did not instantly accept my offer to take Susila to the hospital. To have done so would have been to admit that they had given up all but the slenderest hope of her survival. In the end they did come to me; mostly they had given up hope.

They came back to the bungalow after about half an hour, carrying Susila on the charpoy, wrapped in a cotton shawl, and placed her in the back of the van. Her mother and her father and another person (I think a woman) got in the back with her, and Jodu, the postmaster, sat in the cab with me. I let down the canvas flap at the rear to shut out some of the dust that vacuumed itself into the van on dirt roads. The distance by road from Bisipara to Phulbani is a little over eight miles, two of them along a feeder road and six on the highroad (like the feeder road, unpaved). The feeder road had to be taken at not much more than walking pace, because the Public Works Department had recently engaged a contractor to repair it. The road is repaired each year after the rains. Clods of hard-baked earth are dumped on it to replace that washed away. Bullock carts, the occasional truck, and sometimes the next year's rains, substituted for a roller. The main road, which carried more trucks and had a daily bus service, is more quickly flattened down. We made the trip in the normal time, about half an hour.

Phulbani in 1953 had a lot of open space. Off to one side of the main all-weather Berhampur road, which ended there, was a Kond village, Dakpal, quite inconspicuous amid its paddy fields. The town, built on slightly elevated ground appropriated from the people of Dakpal, followed the standard imperial pattern of the British in India; it sorted out the washed from the unwashed (as did the Indians themselves: the main castes in Bisipara each had their own street). One area was reserved for the office and residence of the district collector, the police station and the police lines, the offices and residences of revenue officials and other officials and their lesser personnel, the high school and its dormitory, and, slightly apart, the hospital and the residences of the civil surgeon and his staff. The buildings were, by local standards, imposing; brick-built, whitewashed, tile-roofed, and surrounded by well-watered and well-kept fenced gardens. People encountered outside, walking from one building to another, were likely to be uniformed, lesser people (constables or peons) wearing turbans and their superiors under solar topees. Officials wore bush jackets or Nehru jackets or, in the case of older senior men or on grand occasions, suits and ties. The impression conveyed— partly accurate and certainly intended—was one of discipline, order, authority, and hierarchy.

The other part of the town was not like that. On the right of the road (driving north from the direction of Berhampur and Bisipara), before one reached the region of symbolized orderliness, there was an area about the size of a football field, sloping gently upward, and lined on two of its sides (north and south) with a higgledy-piggledy array of buildings, of irregular height and dimensions, tin or tile or thatched roofs, mud-plastered walls, a few whitewashed but most the same earthen color as village houses. There were no gardens. All the bigger buildings were shops or storehouses (godowns). In the lesser houses lived people who worked for shopkeepers, who were in small commerce for themselves, or who had menial government jobs that did not entitle them to living quarters. This area was the marketplace, Hatopodera. Every Wednesday the central area would fill with buyers and sellers, a thousand or more; some were professional traders who traveled from market to market, others ordinary people who came in from the hinterland to sell their produce. There was a line of barbers, a line of stalls selling iron tools, others selling clay pots, or (separately) brass pots and aluminum pots, weavers and vendors of cloth, tea stalls (called "hotels"), sellers of puffed rice and other snacks, and two men butchering goats and offering standard leaf-wrapped parcels of meat (a bit of every portion, including organ meats, brains, and even skin). Each commodity or service had its own allotted section in the marketplace. Top center, alone on the east side of the area, was a temple, and, as I recall, another on the north side in the line of shops and houses. The west side, adjoining the road, was open. Compared with that of the official area, the architecture of the marketplace seemed to signify squalor and disorder. On Wednesday, market day, this impression was replaced, as in any open market, by a pleasing sense of the multitudes and their infinite variety and vitality—again in contrast to the inert and standardized government "lines."

Jodu, beside me in the cab, had us halt when we came abreast of Hatopodera, before reaching the hospital. He got out and hurried to a shop about fifty yards up the slope and came back, after a few minutes, with a Bisipara man whom I knew. His name was Basu Pradhan and he was by caste a Distiller. Basu sat up front with us, squeezing himself onto the bench seat, having to hold his dhoti aside from the gear shift. He was a man of substance, a plump man, a shopkeeper first in Bisipara and then in Phulbani, who had expanded his business by taking government contracts to feed prisoners in the jail and later more lucrative contracts with the Public Works Department to repair or construct roads and buildings and other government properties. Life got better for small contractors after 1947, when India gained her independence, for until that time road repairs and other works were often done by unpaid labor extracted from villagers in the neighborhood, on the grounds that they would be the beneficiaries of the work done. Several years on, about 1957 or 1958, Basu was elected chairman of Bisipara's newly established local government body (also called a panchayat). Bisipara people had ambivalent feelings about him and about the caste to which he belonged (the Distillers). People who did not stay in the place that tradition marked out for them made most villagers feel uneasy. Basu's time in office was not a marked success; they thought he used his chairmanship to line his pockets.

Nevertheless, on this day Susila's father and Jodu had no hesitation about enlisting him to help them handle officialdom. Bisipara people had very clear ideas about the role of government and how to deal with it. Where I live now, in California, people are sometimes mildly astonished when they get impeccable service from a bureaucracy, despite having no familiarity with its procedures or with the persons who do the work. We know bureaucracies should work that way; but we are still agreeably surprised, or relieved, when in fact they do. People in Bisipara in 1953 would have been utterly astounded if they had been given that kind of service. It was not that they had any principled quarrel with the idea of governmental authority; they surely would have thought the Reaganesque "government off our backs" a piece of egregious and probably self-serving nonsense. A world bereft of authority, of government, which they called the *raj*, would have been unthinkable; the problem was not how to dispense with government, but how to make good use of it.

Nor did they see government in the pattern of Max Weber's nightmare, as a relentlessly expanding machine that had in it no humanity. Government for them was a collection of individuals who could be manipulated, one way or another, into doing a favor. They had by now heard politicians speak of government as the servant of the people (they voted for the first time in Bisipara in 1952), and they accepted it as empty (and rather incomprehensible) rhetoric. Favors, they believed, went only to those who could pull the right string. They thought I could pull a string for them. Even allowing for the technical convenience of motor transport, I do not think they would have contemplated going to the Phulbani hospital without also having the tacit promise of my intervention. I knew the district commissioner (as it happened another anthropologist with a doctorate from an American university, then recruited into the Indian Administrative Service), and through him I had met his relative, the civil surgeon. The villagers did not know these details. It was enough that I was white-skinned, for this was barely six years after the British had gone from India, and there was everywhere among ordinary people the firmest of impressions that white people could not fail to have influence. (What influence I had, it should be said, came partly from the extraordinary magnanimity of several people who had come to power in Orissa after spending a part of their lives, under British rule, as political prisoners.)

The villagers had a clear idea of how such matters should be arranged. They thought my presence would help, and indeed it did, for the civil surgeon himself got up from his afternoon sleep and ordered an "injection" to be given. I thought Basu was there as the backup, and he was, but not in case I failed. We turned out to be a team. I was to get favors from the people who gave the orders; he was there to see that the people who received the orders found it worth their while to carry them out. I do not, I say again, think that any anticipated foot-dragging or the inevitable incivility from officials and lesser employees lay behind the villagers' initial hesitation to let me take Susila to the hospital. In their place I surely would have been hesitant; I find myself intimidated by the prospect of trying to make reluctant and disobliging administrators disgorge, and certainly angered by the ethical discrepancy between bureaucratic design, which is service, and the actuality of bureaucratic indifference and the sometimes wanton exercise of power.

Bisipara people, I believe, were less judgmental and more real-istic. Romesh's father, Kopilo, provides an instance. He was a schoolmaster. He also worked as my pandit, teaching me to speak Oriya. He was of pensionable age but still employed at the Bisi-para school, where they were short-handed. In recent years he had been summoned, annually, to the office of the inspector of schools in Phulbani to discuss the question of his retirement. Kopilo presented himself at the due time and always sweetened the meeting by taking a gift. The cost in October 1953 was eight rupees. Kopilo considered he had done well, for he had antici-pated being asked for ten rupees. In general, people were con-fident that when they had the resources they could make the system work for them; if they did not have the resources, there would be no point in trying. Their problem was that usually they did not have the resources. On this occasion, however, com-manding the services of both Basu and myself, they may have thought themselves in luck.

Of course in the end there was no good outcome. Drinking tea in the civil surgeon's residence, I asked, breaking into the small talk, what were the girl's prospects. He looked surprised and said, "But she is moribund. It is cerebral malaria. She will die today. What to do? They always come too late. The injection will do nothing. I just gave it to oblige." Whether the favor was done for me or out of compassion for the relatives I do not know. I left about half an hour later with the impression that he thought me remiss not to have known this all along, and that I should not have brought her in. I suppose he was right; all I had done was add another name to the list of those whose fate confirmed that government hospitals and death go together.

Basu took a ride with me—a very short one—back to the marketplace, and I returned to the village alone. The others stayed. I had expected them to, not only because Susila was des-perately ill, but also because, in Indian hospitals of this kind, relatives feed and nurse the patients. A line of simple one-roomed shelters had been built in the hospital compound to accommo-date them.

Next day, around one o'clock in the morning, I was awakened by the noise of women keening. The sound they make is very distinctive, quite different from the crying that occasionally I heard from people hurt or in a rage. The lament (there are words but made mostly incomprehensible by the wailing) announces a death. Sometimes it is the death of a relative in another village. Hearing the lament, people hasten into the street to find out who it is that died. A mischievous adolescent boy, a Warrior, could make the sound to perfection, and he would sometimes hide in a garden or behind a shed and wail and then sneak back into the street to enjoy the confusion of the women who came running.

Later, about four o'clock in the morning, I heard men shouting and got up to see what was going on. Seventy yards away, across the open space behind the bungalow, near the shed that served as a garage, I could see in the light of storm lanterns a group of men assembled on a pathway that went from Warrior street to join a cart track leading to the old ford over the Salki river. To the right of this track, as one came down to the river, was a flat, rockstrewn, untilled area, which had two uses. People went there to defecate, the river being conveniently near to clean oneself afterward. It was also the cremation ground, where, until the monsoon broke and washed everything clean, one came across heaps of ash and fragments of bone.

This party of men, I worked out later, had assembled to build Susila's funeral pyre. She had died at about eleven o'clock the previous night. They secured her body to the charpoy, and four men at a time carried it back from the hospital in Phulbani to Bisipara. They traveled in the night, no doubt shouting as they always did, following the road for five miles and then taking a footpath through the fields and the forest and across the dried-up river bed. I have no note of who they were or of how many men went from Bisipara when the news came back that Susila was dead, but I know that all of them would have been of the Warrior caste and probably of the postmaster's faction because Susila's father was of that caste and that faction. No one else but a Warrior would—or should—come into contact with the body, except perhaps hospital personnel, who did not count in the purity-pollution reckoning. Purity and impurity switch on and off to suit the occasion. Examining wounds or sores, or taking temperatures when people came for medicine, I could touch anyone, high or low caste, male or female, with no fear of giving offense. Outside that context, touching would have been most improper. Various contexts intensify awareness of purity and pollution. A kitchen and the ambience of food is one; the elimination of bodily wastes is another; so also, very strongly, is the ultimate waste product, a corpse.

When the men reached the village they carried Susila's body to the track that ran beside the cremation ground. They set it down and watched over it, guarding it from jackals and hyenas and the village dogs, until there was light enough to build a funeral pyre. When I got up the next morning, Romesh told me that Susila's body had already been cremated. They could cremate her, Kopilo later explained, because there were many men in that family and plenty of hands to bring wood. They burned Susila's corpse on Thursday, March 19.

Over the years I have several times reflected on those events, and, despite the confusedness of my thinking, I can see a pattern in how it developed. While I still lived in Bisipara, and especially on a few subsequent occasions when other people I knew died before their time, my underlying feeling was always that with proper medical care these tragedies would not have happened. In a straightforward way I had faith in Western medicine and a thoroughly commonsensical outlook on the causes of things. If Susila had been taking Paludrine she would not have died. If I had known how to give injections and been on the spot soon enough, she need not have died. About thirty miles away there was a mission hospital, and if one of the doctors had been visiting us, as they sometimes did, she might not have died. If the mosquito eradication program had been further along, she might not have died. (In 1953 it was not yet well known that pesticides may bring along their own perils.) In other words, I thought I lived in a world in which science was triumphant—or would be if things were better arranged. Paludrine cures malaria; saline solutions will cure festering sores. Science gives control over the world, it seemed; it tells us why things happen, how to make them happen, and how to prevent them from happening.

What I did not see was how very limited in practice, and how very uncertain, and at times (conversely) how dangerous, this control was. Even when the theory was right, as seems to have been the case with whatever theory underlies Paludrine, the proportion of events in the real world influenced by the theory's application was minuscule. Of course, science may work the other way; there are applications with momentous and regrettable consequences, as in the case of nuclear fission. DDT, much in vogue in 1953, also shows that things can go wrong. But at that time and in that place I had a more or less unthinking faith in my own scientific culture, when set against the culture of the people in Bisipara. I thought of Susila and of what injections might have done. I thought, in the same vein but more light-heartedly, that with a bulldozer I could make a level paddy field out of an uneven sloping patch of ground in half a day, when it took Jodu and the men working for him several months. Now I could write a book on the awful unintended consequences that would have followed if I had owned a bulldozer as well as an Austin van.

Later reflection brought some humility, a blurring of the boundaries between their thinking and mine. I had a professional interest in some of the things that they did in the sickroom, and still more in the events that I will describe as the story unfolds in later chapters. What was done gave me an insight into the way minds in Bisipara worked, and into how different their style of thinking was from my (scientific) style. I did not have the same insight into the meaning of what *I* did. I noted the aromatic leaves being burned under the bed in the room and thought that not only did the smoke make breathing difficult but also it could in no way relieve, let alone cure, the girl's fever. I knew later that the amulet around her neck was there for her protection; but that could at best have had a psychological effect, and by the time I saw her she was clearly beyond the reach of suggestion. I knew that the

Preparing a paddy field for planting. The plank, drawn by water buffalos, levels and homogenizes the liquid mud. The field belongs to the sirdar. The laborer, hired for the season, is a Kond.

man feeding the fire was a gunia, a diviner, expert in dealing with cases of possession. But, when I heard the carpenter say that this was a sickness, it was not a case of possession, I tacitly agreed and concluded that the gunia in reality had nothing to offer. Demons may attack people, in a metaphorical sense; I saw that in Bisipara and I have seen it elsewhere. But they do not attack people by inflicting malaria; in that domain there are no demons. Furthermore, if Susila had got better, it would not have been the result of aromatic smoke, or amulets, or whatever magic the gunia might have performed, because those things have no basis in hard science.

Is that how the people of Bisipara made the division? Did Syamo call in the gunia as the representative of magic and me as representing science? I am sure not; those are my categories. For the girl's parents and kinsmen there must have been just one category marked by the criterion of "Maybe they have a remedy." (I learned later that the headmaster of Bisipara's upper primary school, a Brahmin from another village, had come to the house to cast Susila's horoscope, in the hope that it might help them work out what was to be done.) Maybe cost entered at the margin of their calculations; people in Bisipara are no less rational than in other places. Certainly risk did, as in the reckoning that people who go to the government hospital often die. But they did not see me and the civil surgeon as the owners of a distinct and exclusively valid brand of truth. The realization that their thinking did not have to be like mine came to me almost at once, for in anthropology that notion was then and still is a cornerstone. It was harder to suppress the habit of assuming that my ideas were better.

There is an irony in this remembering of my own culture's superiority. Medical skills in my childhood in Britain were surely better than those available to the people of Bisipara two decades later, certainly better than in the days of my grandparents, when infant deaths were normal events. In my childhood the saving regimen of hygiene ruled, as it had not earlier and as it still did not in Bisipara. But illness, especially childhood illness, in the

1920s and 1930s and still in wartime had an almost Bisipara-like quality of uncertainty about it. Infections were not quickly controlled by antibiotics, as happens now, nor were all of them preventable by inoculation. Children died of measles and whooping cough. They died of tuberculosis. They died of poliomyelitis. The children's hospital had isolation wards for diphtheria and scarlet fever. Pneumonia was not uncommon, and its mythology spoke of the "crisis," the moment of the body's decision between life and death. Being treated amounted to little more than being put to bed, and nursed and nourished, in the hope that the body's natural defenses would assert themselves. In that respect we did little more for illness than they were able to do in Bisipara in the 1950s.

What I did not realize, when Susila fell ill, was how very unscientific in style were my own actions. My motivation was consciously scientific—Paludrine cures fever, and my task was to bring down the girl's fever—but the significance of my actions, to myself much later but probably to the others at the time I did them, was quite otherwise. Certainly my efforts with Paludrine had no more effect than the amulet or the aromatic smoke or the headmaster's Brahminic expertise or whatever the gunia may have done. In trying to administer tablets, even ground in water, to a patient incapable of swallowing, I was doing nothing of medical significance. The truth was, I later realized, that the meaning of what I did was no different from the injection given by the civil surgeon. I was doing it "to oblige." More precisely, I was signaling my distress and my desire to help, my concern that such tragic events should have come about, and my common humanity with the girl and her family. I was doing that in addition to—and surely more effectively than—attempting to practice medicine.

2

Kith and Kin

A household is a private domain, and the family in it live inward toward the courtyard, behind the blank walls that face the street. The street is a public place, where men sit and gossip when they have no work to do. Small children, boys and girls, play around them. Women do not linger in the street, for the conventions of the village lay down that women have no public life. Their gossiping is done in the courtyards, or across garden fences behind the houses, or when they go down to the river to take a bath. Sometimes three or four of them go off together, carrying small brass pots of water on their heads, to chat while they defecate in a field (after the harvest is in), or on the river bank, or in the wasteland where they burn the dead.

All houses have verandas, both in the courtyard and on the street side, earthen platforms two feet high, the grandest of them about a yard wide. Their surfaces are plastered with the mixture of earth and cow dung, polished smooth by contact with men's feet and bodies, and always swept (by women) as clean as the floors inside the house. There men sit to watch their world go by, drawing up their legs when the lumbering cattle are driven past, morning and evening, by the village Herdsman. They talk to friends, sitting side by side at the edge or sometimes squatting back against the wall to avoid the sun. On cold winter mornings they wrap themselves in cotton shawls and perch like a row of

birds to catch the warmth of the early sun. Men of lower status—
for example, untouchables who have news to bring or business
to be done in Warrior street—do not share the veranda but sit
on their heels in the dirt of the street. Good manners command
them to do so, for if they were standing, the socially superior
person would have to look up to them. Besides, the veranda is on
the margins of the household, and untouchables may not enter a
"pure" house without good reason.

On the morning of March 19 (the day of Susila's cremation) I
was sitting on the sirdar's veranda, as I often did, doing nothing.
I saw a man carrying six new clay cooking pots, slung three to a
net at each end of a bamboo pole balanced on his right shoulder,
and walking with that curiously fast rhythmic gait that matches
the flexing of the bamboo. (The bounce seems to make the load
lighter; I tried it.) Pots, about a foot tall and the same in diameter,
are unglazed and blackened from the straw fires in which they
are baked. The man, a stranger to me, had come from the village
of Gonjagura, a mile away across the river, where the Potters (unlike those in Bisipara) still made pots. This information I got from
Jaya, the sirdar's eldest son, who had come out to sit beside me.
The Potter went past us and turned into the compound where
Susila had lived.

A little later I heard the sound of women wailing, and a procession of them came out of Susila's compound, some carrying
clay cooking pots, old ones that would be replaced by the Gonjagura man's delivery. I recognized Susila's mother and a few other
women, but not many because they moved away from us up the
street toward a pathway that led to the river. They walked very
slowly, always keening. Others joined the group until there were
about forty women, wailing, clustered around Susila's mother.
Beside the pathway, as it emerges behind the houses, is a place
where old cooking pots are deliberately smashed when a household has to be cleansed. Pots are smashed at the first-fruits ritual,
as a symbol of renewal; when a child is born and the household is
polluted for twenty-one days; and to purify a house when someone has died. I heard the pots from Susila's house being broken.

About twenty minutes later a dozen or so women came back, still wailing, and went into Susila's compound. The rest of the group, I suppose, had gone directly to their own houses. The women had washed themselves in the river. Wet saris, the short knee-length kind that village women wore, clung to their bodies, and their long black hair lay uncoiled and disordered around their shoulders. Jaya politely turned his head away.

Almost all the women who had gone down to the river had been born in other villages and had come to Bisipara in marriage. Girls whom Jaya called "sister" or "father's sister" (whether or not they were Warriors and therefore his actual or potential relatives) went elsewhere in marriage. Marriages, virtually always arranged, were sometimes contracted between children, but girls did not join their husbands until they were sexually mature, usually about sixteen or seventeen, Susila's age. Consequently, with the exception of a handful of women who had been divorced and had no children and had come back to live with brothers or the father, mature women living in Bisipara had been born elsewhere. The women who escorted Susila's mother down to the river and almost all the other married women in the village, being incomers, were ranked below the men. But in a quite literal sense the men, who (without even thinking about it) knew themselves to be the essence of the community, depended on these women for the community's continued existence; the core group could not breed on its own sisters. Incoming women, nevertheless, were seen in public life as secondary, peripheral, and sometimes as a threat.

When the Gonjagura man brought the pots and the women came out of Susila's house, Jaya set about explaining to me what was going on. I listened, not interrupting, but I already knew what they were doing. Between February 17 and March 20 six people died in Bisipara. (There may have been other deaths, unknown to me.) Of two deaths, both in Distiller families, occurring between March 13 and March 20, I have only a note that "Banamali's infant son and Madhu Sahu's old mother died." I knew the two men, but I have no record of the death rituals that must have followed. The deaths of infant children mostly go without comment, and no one would have told me about them, unless there were some reason for doing so. Women wail, of course, but hardly a day seemed to go by without my hearing that sound, and I soon got in the habit of assuming that the death was in some other place and that if it was not, I would hear about it sooner or later.

I did hear directly about the death of one small child, because Romesh was involved. Romesh belonged to the Herdsman caste. His father, Kopilo, the schoolmaster, now widowed, had married into one of the other Hersdsman families in Bisipara. The three brothers, who in 1953 constituted the core of that family, although of the same generation as Romesh in our way of reckoning relationships, stood to him in the Bisipara idiom as "mother's brothers." He, as sister's son, was their *jati puo* (literally, "caste son"). In that capacity he had specific duties to perform when there was a death in his uncles' house. On March 1 he came early to say that he would be absent for a couple of hours that morning. The small son of the eldest of the three brothers had died in the night. No one knew why. They just woke up and found him dead. One of the younger brothers came to tell Romesh (they lived at opposite ends of Warrior street). Romesh and the two younger brothers and another young man, who was employed by the village to herd its cattle, wrapped the child's body in a cloth and took it to the forest and buried it. As they filled the grave they put in thorn bushes and they piled rocks on the top to discourage hyenas from unearthing it. (Out walking, I stumbled over one of these places. The hyenas get what they are after.) The four men took a bath in the river on their way back and then made a fire and threw lime leaves on it, inhaling the smoke to purify themselves.

The older women in the house of the three brothers were both widows. One was the mother of the three men and the other was a childless old woman, by name Rua, of quite remarkable acerbity (at a wedding I attended in that house I had seen her reduce a young woman to tears). She was the widow of the paternal uncle of the three brothers. Rua gathered up the pots and took them out to smash and then she and her sister-in-law and a woman from the Washerman household took the dead child's mother down to the river and bathed her. When they came back they threw lime leaves on the fire, so that, Romesh said, the smoke would remove the aroma of death, because death-laden air is harmful to those who breath it; it makes them ill.

At that time the house was still polluted and no cooking could be done there. Household stocks of food could be used, but the preparation must be done by a jati puo, in his own house. The food is then carried to the bereaved. On this occasion Romesh's wife cooked a meal of rice and dal, garnishing the rice with lime leaves. Romesh carried it to them. There are other restrictions, besides cooking, during the mourning period. It is not appropriate to initiate anything auspicious; celebratory festivals, such as a marriage or a betrothal ceremony or even villagewide rituals, should be postponed until the taint of death has been removed. This removal is accomplished through a series of rituals culminating in a ceremony called *sraddha*.

The sraddha for the dead Herdsman boy was performed on the sixth day after his death. There is a time schedule, adjusted according to the status of the deceased. If a child dies at the moment of birth or within a day or two afterward, the mourning lasts three days and no one else is likely to be involved except the immediate household. A child who has lived longer, especially a boy (convention cares less about small girls), commands six days before the sraddha. That rule applies up to the time that marriage converts the youth into an adult. After that he is mourned for twelve days. A woman who has gone in marriage to another village is mourned for six days. That also is the proper period for a girl like Susila, betrothed but not yet departed to her husband's house. A woman married into Bisipara will be mourned for twelve days. The principle is clear enough: the length of mourning is adjusted to the importance of the deceased, assessed Bisipara-style by the criteria of age, gender, and marital status.

A similar rule decides which households will be involved in

Jaya, the sirdar's eldest son, is hoisted and danced on the shoulders of his father's Kond subjects. The occasion is Jaya's wedding.

the mourning and what role they will play in it. The grades are no less clear; agnatically related households (those linked by descent through their male heads) are maximally disabled by a death. Households related through women also mourn but are less disabled; indeed, they are the ones who cook for the bereaved households. In a village like Bisipara those two categories are likely to cover everyone in any particular caste. People of other castes, by definition not kinfolk, show their concern by giving lesser forms of help, for example bringing wood for the pyre or helping dig a grave and, when the death is that of an adult man or woman, contributing in cash or kind to the expenses of the feast that marks a sraddha.

I have accounts for some of those feasts, and it is clear that they are grand occasions. On Tuesday, March 10, an aged man of the Warrior caste, called Kola Bisoi, inconveniently died. His death was inconvenient because it occurred at the climax of a three-day celebration for Jaya's wedding. Because Jaya was the eldest son of the sirdar, this wedding was a formidable affair, attended by more than a thousand guests, who were being feasted on the night of March 10. The news of Kola's death was kept quiet until after the feast was done. Several men, including the young man who inherited Kola's land (neither Kola himself nor Mithu, the heir, had been able to spell out the genealogical link between them), took the body to the forest and buried it.

Ten days after the death of Kola, the principal mourner, Mithu, was taken to the river, bathed, and had his head shaved by a man from the Barber caste. A Brahmin conducted a ceremony in which ten small cakes made from flour and ten small portions of cooked rice were consecrated and consumed. When that was done, all those present put on new clean clothes. On the twelfth day the sraddha was held. After that, the period of pollution was ended and the household and others who had been joined in mourning were free to resume their normal lives.

I have the accounts of the feast that marked Kola's sraddha. Note that neither Kola nor Mithu was wealthy. The feast, held at noon on March 22, seemed to me, as all these large affairs in Bisipara did, a logistical feat. It was organized in three sectors. First, male relatives from other villages and Bisipara men of the Warrior caste who belonged to the sirdar's faction (as Kola had and Mithu did) sat down to be fed. Separate from them, but at the same time, certain privileged people (of castes lower in rank than the Warriors and therefore willing to take cooked food from them) were fed. Women and children were served after the men, portions of food being carried to the individual households. Second, cooked food was distributed to Warrior households of the faction headed by Jodu the postmaster (to which Susila's father belonged). Third, uncooked food was sent to Distiller street and Potter street, and to a cluster of households in Bisipara's market street, Hatopodera, to the masters of the upper primary school, and to ourselves.

The reckoning says that one hundred *tambis* of rice were expended. A tambi is a measure of volume, and one hundred tambis is equivalent to twenty-five gallons of uncooked rice. Bisipara's expectation is that a reasonable eater consumes about one quarter of a tambi (half a pint) at a sitting, which would mean that about four hundred people were feasted. In addition five gallons of lentils were cooked or distributed and seven goats slaughtered. At night another meal was cooked, but only for visiting kin and a few closely related households in Bisipara. This meal required two and a half gallons of rice and half a gallon of lentils. (In 1953 the cost of a gallon of rice varied from one to two rupees, reflecting preharvest scarcity and postharvest plenty. September, October, and early November are the hardest times. The main paddy harvests are reaped first in November and extend into late December or early January. One rupee was then a day's wage for an adult male laborer.)

Funerals are evidently expensive, and if they come too frequently, and especially if they coincide with other disasters (such as the death of an ox), a householder can fall ruinously into debt, borrowing against the security of his land and eventually, perhaps, losing it. But the bereaved do not bear the cost alone. From nine villages kinfolk came to Kola's sraddha, bringing between them about twenty tambis of rice, two goats and several sets of clothing (a man's dhoti, a woman's sari, or the small towel-like shawl they call a *gamucha*). I have a record of thirty tambis of rice, one goat, and several lengths of cloth from individual households in Bisipara, together with a note that two of the streets (Distillers and Potters) each made joint contributions. If these accounts are accurate, Mithu may well have come more than halfway to covering his costs.

Kola's death put seventeen households (about eighty people)

into full mourning. I was prompted to think of this, sitting on the veranda beside Jaya on the morning Susila was cremated, by the sight of the only man in the village who qualified to be jati puo for Jodu the postmaster's faction of Warriors, to which Susila's father belonged. (The jati puo's name was Madhia Behera. His paternal grandfather had married a Bisoi woman and come to live in Bisipara.) He and his wife coped for the first meal, but afterward people related to Syamo's lineage through women came from other villages to take the pressure off him. That morning he walked past us, carrying an enormous brass platter of cooked rice and dal to Susila's house. It prompted me to ask Jaya who had cooked for his household when Kola died. There was no problem, he said. The cooks from his wedding feast stayed on for three days. Then they had his little "sister" (his father's half-brother's daughter, twelve years old) do the cooking; she was already betrothed, and therefore really counted as part of her husband's lineage, and was therefore polluted for the lesser time. The lesser time in fact is six days, not three.

I might have asked him about the discrepancy, but I let it pass because it seemed to be part of a pattern that was emerging. I was beginning to realize that I was too eager to find consistency. I saw myself in search of the authorized version, *the* definitive edition of culture, so to speak, but I kept encountering inconsistencies, between customs or between what people said should be done, or said was done, and what they actually did. These discrepancies made me feel that something was amiss and that it was my task to iron out the inconsistencies and get things into proper intellectual order. If rules and behavior did not conform, I must have been misinformed. If they had customs they surely must follow them, and if they appeared not to do so, I must have misunderstood something. I wanted the Bisipara pattern of life that I was describing to be like the outward appearance of the government lines in Phulbani; everything neat, in order, and wholly predictable. But things did not work that way. The rule said six days; three days was more convenient; so on the fourth day Jaya's little sister did the cooking, and they fudged the rule to make her eligible to do the work. When there is a death the women set to wailing so that everyone may know; but when the sirdar's house was celebrating the wedding of the year—if not of the generation—the women contained themselves until a less inconvenient time. Such creative adjustments, I had not yet realized, are no less a part of culture than a firmly stated rule. Culture is a process of continuing negotiation between the rule and the particular requirements of the situation in which it is to be applied. Moreover, people usually are not obsessive in their search for definitively correct conduct and settle for what is good enough; they live by compromise and are content to do so.

At the time I had not understood this, and their casual attitude toward correct conduct, together with some manifest instances of pretense and hypocrisy, pushed me toward a mildly despairing skepticism. The version that was not "authorized," I assumed, was not authentic, and I began to see fakery everywhere. I had been thinking, on several levels, about grief. I had surely seen anxiety and concern and sorrow on the day that Susila died. In her parents I think I saw grief, the genuine emotion, but I did not know them well, and Bisipara people are immensely reserved and controlled in the presence of outsiders, especially ones with powerful connections. I know I saw real grief in a short conversation I had with a Bisipara woman, when I went back to the village in 1959 and she told me about the death of her son, whom I had last seen when he was about eight. I did not confuse the public showpiece lamentations with grief, but they did give rise to a tacit sense that people who could do that must also be immunized against the genuine emotion. They may not have been the "hired grief" of nineteenth century undertakers in Britain, since the mourners were always relatives of the dead person, but I could not see their grieving as any more authentic. That thinking is obviously confused; but it is how my mind, schooled both to value sincerity and at the same time to question its manifestations, worked.

Chanti, a woman from the Sweeper caste, an untouchable, worked for us in the bungalow. She was cheerful, energetic, a very handsome woman, the second wife of a widower, and coping with a sullen near-teenage stepdaughter and a brood of four young children of her own, all under six. Her husband's elder brother died on February 17. A week later I went to watch their version of the sraddha. In the courtyard five or six women, among them Chanti, were squatting in a line. They were clad in old discolored saris, which they tore from time to time; they also tore at their hair; they threw dirt in their faces; and they were shrieking their grief. They did not see me at first. Chanti was weeping and howling and pulling at her hair and rending her sari, with the result that her breasts were uncovered. Then she saw me, and that was the occasion when my camera caught her pulling the remnants of her sari across her breasts and aiming the brightest of smiles at the lens. A few moments later she was back at her wailing.

I also found myself put out, again illogically, by inept ritual performances. I knew they were inept only because the performers were being scolded and corrected. On March 17 (the day on which Susila was taken ill) I was present at a ritual intended to place Chanti's dead brother-in-law among his ancestors. It was performed by the dead man's daughter-in-law, who was directed at every step by one of six men who squatted around her, criticizing her every move. On such occasions I kept looking for reverence, for an awareness of the divine presence, at least a respect for the occasion; but there seemed to be none. Six days before the Herdsman child died, his young uncle married. At a crucial part of the ceremony, as the bride and groom circled the fire (the god Agni), the Brahmin priest stopped and said he would not do another thing until they promised to pay him more money. There was a haggle between the priest and the groom's eldest brother. The fire burned low, and the bride and groom squatted patiently down to await the outcome. The Brahmin's fee was fractionally raised, they threw some slivers of aromatic wood on the fire, and the ceremony got under way again. No one seemed surprised or put out by the incident.

My mistake, I see now, was looking for the kind of impeccable order that is found when people really do "go by the book," when the loose guide of custom has been systematized into regulations or when rituals have been formalized into audience-conscious theater. People in communities like Bisipara mostly do not run their lives that way. They often pretend to be closely constrained by custom; but the truth is that Bisipara people, like people in many other places, turn out to be sticklers for rules only when it suits them.

The misfortunes of Kopilo, Romesh's father, provide an instance. Still employed as a teacher, and working for me, he was doing well financially. One day, in August 1955, he came to borrow an advance against his salary. (All those who worked regularly for us in Bisipara maneuvered themselves through advances into a position where I would lose money if I dismissed them. None of them, so far as I could tell, took advantage of me by shirking. They saw themselves, I suspect, in what to me is an unlikely mixture of the commercial and the familial, both as employees and as loyal retainers in my household.) I asked why he needed the money now. The panchayat, he said, had fined him twenty-five rupees. At that time the monsoon was late, and the village was employing ritual specialists of several kinds to make it rain. They were also looking for people to blame for stopping the rain. The offenders, people who had defied dharma, the natural order of things, could be fined and the fines used to pay for the specialists. They found a variety of culprits who had upset the order of things, including Kopilo. What had this frail, nearly blind old man, in his mid-sixties, done? He had had an affair with his deceased wife's younger brother's wife, herself a widow. He had addressed her husband as "younger brother," and to have sexual connection with a younger brother's wife is, in Bisipara reckoning, incestuous and pollutes the earth. That is one way to stop the rains from coming. I looked at him in wonder, and the wonder grew when he told me that the lady concerned was that ancient shrew, Rua the widow. Then it came clear; all this had happened twenty or more years earlier. Evidently it had been stored in the community's memory, waiting for a time when it could be put to use.

They also picked out a Brahmin who two years earlier had seduced his brother's wife, but he ran away before they could extract any money out of him. They found several other pigeons, not all of them adulterers. For example, a woman who touched a plow thereby polluted the earth. They dredged up two cases. One, a Herdsman widow, about five years earlier had been correcting the hold her twelve-year-old son had on the plow's handle. She was poor, and they demanded no more than a token fine from her. The other, more recent, was a young Distiller wife in Nuasai who had picked up a plow (they are wooden and not excessively heavy) and carried it out of her house. It was an emergency; the house was on fire. But that did not alter the case; her father-in-law, Sripati Pradhan, paid a modest fine.

My immediate reaction was cynicism. Here was no true-belief; only opportunism, the kind of truth manipulation through selective recall of past events that was manifested in the American presidential election of 1992. The matter had nothing to do with polluting the earth and holding back the rains; someone wanted money and thought that Kopilo and the other offenders could be made to pay.

Only the second part of that sentence can stand the test of time. The first part is a miniature of the uncertainty that underlies my interpretation of this entire story about Susila's death. Perhaps Bisipara people did believe that Kopilo's indiscretions had something to do with polluting the earth and holding back the rains. Certainly they did not allow women to plow. But the cynicism of forty years ago at least made one thing clear. A neat and tidy description of custom, in the sense of the rules that people said should be followed, would be quite unrealistic. Rules were being bent and broken all the time. Certainly one would need to know what the rules were; but they were by no means descriptions of what people actually did. Nor were they a reliable guide to what they really believed. More often they were the claims that people made to justify what they were about to do or what they had done.

There is one more twist to this pattern of thought. While part of my mind took in the manifest pretense, the occasionally patent hypocrisy, and always the casual flexibility with which rules and customs were interpreted, the other part was very much impressed with the way in which things actually did get done in Bisipara. I estimate that four hundred people were fed at Kola's sraddha. At least a thousand were feasted at Jaya's wedding. Every year the village put on a fourteen-day-and-night nonstop dramatic performance, climaxing it with a hugely attended festival. I was also impressed with the fact that no one stood alone, neither in sorrow nor in joy; a community of people—family, caste, village—was always at hand, whether called or not. People rarely slipped through the mesh, whether the net was put out to capture them or to save them. The other side, of course, is that neither did anyone have privacy of the kind that is valued in our society; we believe we have the right to tell the collectivity— the state or the community or the public in general—that it is trespassing and to warn it off.

Bisipara people did have ways of dealing with busybodies. Certain situations were, by convention, private. When women went off to defecate together they did so within earshot, but each in a private place, not gazing at one another. (They did not go so far as the missionary ladies we knew who, preparing themselves for a visit to their privyless converts, sang hymns loudly to drown out the noise they made peeing on dry leaves in the forest.) The same parts of the body that are private among us are also private there. A woman's breasts are often accidently revealed, since they do not wear blouses, but no grown man should gaze at them. Eating is an intensely private activity. The most persistent callers at the bungalow—those who assumed that they would not get the medicine or whatever else they wanted unless they were resolutely importunate, as they would have to be at a government office—would immediately retire and wait fifty yards away if Romesh told them we were eating. The rationale is the

evil eye; food is made harmful if someone looks at it. Men do not
face each other at a feast; they sit side by side in a line. Anything
that might cause envy—a handsome baby, for example—should
never be made the object of praise or, indeed, looked at overtly
and directly.

Privacy, they believe, is also violated by asking for certain kinds
of information. Yet they did it all the time. I recall walking with
Debohari, another Bisoi and a younger "brother" of the sirdar
(they shared a common great-grandfather). He had been to the
store in Warrior street and bought a length of cloth. The four
people whom we met (all men) stopped, fingered the cloth, and
asked what he had paid. The appropriate answer, which seemed
to be acceptable, was "Who knows?" If, as I often did when we
were making field maps, I walked in the company of Jaya or
Debohari along one of the paths that led out to the paddy fields,
we would be asked, routinely, "Where are you going?" The correct answer is "Just taking a stroll." The convention seems to be
that one has a right to ask but not a right to be told. The ability to
refuse and restrict interaction is in fact a way of staying sane in
close communities. Community life exists on secrets and privacy,
just as it also exists on Ibsen's lies.

Events and my reflections about them had confronted me with
the tension that, in varying degrees, is everywhere present between individual rights and the collectivity on which individuals
depend. The Bisipara collectivity flexed its muscles, but only a
little, that same day (March 19) on which Susila had been cremated and I spent the morning sitting on Jaya's veranda watching people come and go. In the evening there was a meeting of
the panchayat held to confirm arrangements for Ramnobomi, the
two-week dramatic performance to celebrate the life of the god
Sri Ramchandro. The recitations were due to begin the following Monday, which was March 23. On that day the community
would have to be in an appropriately auspicious condition, untainted by any evil force. Otherwise, there was a risk that the
festival would go wrong.

The panchayat existed to make sure that village affairs ran

smoothly and to set them on the right track when they went
wrong, which they often did. People who had a quarrel came
before the panchayat to have their differences settled. The panchayat organized the many festivals that enlivened the village
year. It was also the major arena in which the judicial contests
that followed Susila's death were played out. The panchayat was
in some ways like a parliament or an assembly in which those
who in fact wielded power were obliged to observe the forms of
equality and brotherhood with their less powerful fellows and
to clothe naked self-interest in the garb of concern for the public good.

The panchayat meetings were held in the building they called
the *mandap*. My Oriya dictionary translates that word as "pan-
dal," which is a "temporary shed used for meetings." Bisipara's
mandap was indeed used for meetings, but it was also a very
solid and permanent construction. It sat in the middle of Warrior street, between the two lines of houses, slightly west of the
sirdar's compound on the south side of the street and Jodu the
postmaster's house on the north.

The panchayat held almost all its meetings there, unless they
had to hear a case in which women or untouchables would be
present as plaintiffs, defendants, or witnesses. Then they would
meet outside in the shade of one of the several large trees that
grew on the edges of Bisipara. The reason for going outside, Jaya
explained, was that the mandap was a temple, and its precincts
were restricted to men of clean caste. They could still meet in the
mandap if a case involved just one or two people ineligible to
come inside, for those people could stand outside in the street
and shout whatever they had to say. The architecture of the mandap made this arrangement possible, if somewhat inconvenient,
for excluded litigants. On the one hand the walls were open, the
substantial thatched roof being supported on wooden pillars a
foot or more in diameter. It was easy enough, if people raised
their voices, for litigants standing in the street to be heard and for
them to hear the comments and deliberations inside the building.

On the other hand, the floor of the mandap was five feet above
street level. (It was reached from the eastern end by a wide flight
of wooden steps.) Those compelled to remain in the street and
still wanting to hear what was going on had to stand, a posture
Bisipara people do not find comfortable; they prefer to sit on their
heels. Most excluded litigants tried to find a panchayat member
to speak on their behalf.

A small part of the mandap, at the western end, was closely
fenced on four sides with vertical poles set a few inches apart.
Inside could be seen drums and various weapons, the paraphernalia of wars that had been fought more than a century earlier,
before the region was pacified. This precinct was a shrine for the
tutelary deity of the lordly Warriors, and therefore of the village.
The larger part of the building, to the east, served not only as a
meeting place for the panchayat, but also as a dormitory for men.
Visitors might spend the night there. Adolescent boys, whose
presence at home was considered inconvenient, would be sent
to sleep there. Married men, too, sometimes chose to take refuge
there. Dormitories of this kind, architecturally very similar, are
found throughout the Kond hills. But in Kond villages they are
places of courtship, the preserve of the young and unmarried.
Village girls sleep there and are joined by parties of boys who
come from other villages. (Boys and girls in the same village are
likely to be related in such a way that lovemaking would be considered incestuous.) Bisipara's mandap, however, like those in
other Oriya-speaking villages, was an exclusively male domain.

A panchayat, if the word is taken literally, is an assembly of
five males, said to incorporate, in some mysterious fashion, the
wisdom of God into its decisions. In that way the worldly differences in power and influence between panchayat members
was subsumed in their collective participation in the divinity;
being one with God, all were equal. In Bisipara the panchayat
comprised the male heads of all households of clean caste. That
meant mostly Warriors, Distillers, and Potters, together with two
or three households (each) of Herdsmen, Brahmins, Barbers, the

single household of Washermen, and sundry others. Excluded were numerous households of Panos, an untouchable caste, and the single compound of Sweepers, also untouchables.

The rule confining membership to heads of households was somewhat flexible. Married men in a joint household attended as of right, and I often saw young unmarried men present, for example the sirdar's son Jaya before his marriage, and Suren, Jodu's grown but then unmarried son. Both these boys had been to high school in Phulbani, and their services were occasionally enlisted to write something down. A lot of the middle-aged men could read, and write their names, but they were not practiced with the pen as the young men were. Unmarried men, however, rarely spoke in the panchayat unless spoken to. As in other parts of India, young males were expected to be elaborately deferential toward their elders, and their elders were correspondingly imperious. Panchayat meetings were well regulated, those, at least, that I attended. Occasionally I saw someone lose his temper, or appear to do so, but that did not happen often. People took turns speaking. Matters were decided by consensus, a procedure that puzzled me for a long time until I came to appreciate that the consensus was the voice of the divinity. I never saw a vote taken.

The nature of this body eventually became clear to me. It sat as a court to arbitrate or mediate disputes, but its primary task was to manage Bisipara's public affairs. It administered public properties and kept them in repair: the mandap itself, various temples and the fields with which they were endowed, the school building, some parts of the irrigation network, and various other things were under its care. It hired the Sweeper family to clean the streets, a Herdsman to take cattle to the forest and keep them away from growing crops in unfenced fields, a Herdsman widow to pasture the goats, and Brahmins to conduct the many public rituals that had to be performed. It set a standard rate of payment for day laborers hired to work in the fields and attempted, not always with success, to prevent landowners from paying over the rate when, especially during the planting of paddy seedlings (done one by one, by hand), labor was short. As a judicial body, it heard cases of theft or trespass or broken contracts, mediated marital disputes, and many times acted on its own behalf to impose penalties on people who had not contributed work or money demanded by the panchayat or who had not abided by its judicial decisions.

My first image of the panchayat was a combination of a court of law and an administrative committee, a genuine formal organization designed to work by impersonal bureaucratic standards. There was some trace of this feature: meetings had agendas, announced at the beginning; minutes were kept (in a somewhat irregular fashion); a careful record was written of who had paid up and who had not when contributions were levied to reconstruct Sri Ramchandro's temple or to meet the expenses of his annual celebration. I could also detect a Bisipara equivalent of *Robert's Rules of Order* giving shape to their discussions. But there were two other features, one that is shared by similar institutions in our society and one that is not. The first is that the panchayat, in addition to being an administrative and judicial body, was also an arena or a cockpit in which people, while claiming to serve the public interest, in fact were often trying to serve their own. In that respect the panchayat was no different from many committees, councils, and courts in our own society.

The second feature was that the panchayat had no independent executive branch, no officials, to carry out its decisions. There was one person whose task it was to go around and announce that a meeting would be held and to summon people to it or to run messages. He was in fact not the servant of the panchayat but a lackey of the sirdar. (This was one of the village watchmen, a Pano, and therefore not himself entitled to take part in panchayat deliberations.) The members themselves had to be their own executives. The result, it is not difficult to see, was that those who did not like a decision dragged their feet about implementing it.

Open defiance was quite rare, and when it did occur, the panchayat was nonplussed. In October 1953 there was a very noisy quarrel in the middle of the night between some Potters who were drunk. It was so noisy that someone sounded the tocsin (an empty kerosene can hung in each street and beaten with a stick). A posse of annoyed senior men arrived to find out what was going on, convened a meeting, and summoned the offenders, who responded with defiance and insults. But next day, sobered up, they came to the panchayat, apologized, said they did not know what they were doing, and "of their own accord each gave three rupees honor-money to the panchayat," as Debohari put it. But a fourth offender, a man of Writer caste and an outsider employed in the shop, continued to be defiant, said he had not been part of the disturbance, and walked out of the meeting. The panchayat, Debohari reported, "was dumbfounded," and postponed further consideration until the next day. By the next day, the Writer's employer had given him some advice, and he came to the meeting, apologized and paid over "of his own accord" three rupees.

The "proper" form of defiance was to agree to do something and then not do it. (It took me some time to realize that they thought such deception the height of good manners. Only a boor, or someone out to make trouble, or an ignorant and irresponsible outsider like the man from the shop, would be honest about his intentions.) Promises could in fact be broken with some degree of impunity because the panchayat, besides having no executive officers, had no practical sanctions other than the very severe one of denying the offender continued membership of the community. (They had taken over the English word *boycott* for this procedure.) If that was to be done, everyone, of course, had first to agree. If excluded in that way, Susila's father and mother would have sat alone with their other two children and watched her die, and the father alone would have had to carry the body to the forest and bury it, for one man by himself cannot cut enough dry wood to make a funeral pyre. Such a situation was unimaginable, both to me and to the people of Bisipara; severity of that kind defeats itself. A disciplinary system that has social death as its one effective penalty in effect most of the time has no penalty.

The panchayat could, and frequently did, impose fines. But if the offender did not pay up, nothing could be done, short of the extreme penalty, except threaten and nag.

There is another way to look at this arrangement, which makes it seem less bizarre. I soon caught on to it, for it is another commonplace in anthropology (although it is not always easy to recognize in practice what one has known only from theory). Courts of law and bureaucratic procedure in general in our society uphold the rule and are concerned with precedent and think only secondly, if at all, about how the relationships of litigants are going to work out when the case is over and the verdict is handed down. But in Bisipara, as in face-to-face societies everywhere in the world, the primary concern is to restore harmony, or at least a sufficient pretense of harmony so that people can get on with their lives. That is one aspect of the rule of consensus: everyone must agree, for everyone's agreement is the same as social harmony.

The underlying realities of consensus are otherwise. First, as I said, people may agree in their words but not in what they do. Second, the absence of flexible sanctions leads to a kind of bargaining, in which the panchayat attempts to cajole people to agree that they are in the wrong and should be penalized. That spirit of "settle for what you can" continues beyond the verdict, and the man who has agreed to pay a fine of twenty-five rupees may pay five, and nothing more is said.

Third, what appears to be consensus is often a reluctant compliance on the part of those too weak to make a protest. This fact quite turns the picture around. I have given the impression of a collectivity pleading with recalcitrant individuals to do the right thing and subordinate themselves to the public interest. Essentially that picture is correct, but it is not complete. It would indeed be an accurate picture if the members of the panchayat, nominally a group of equal, impartial, and fair-minded men, were in actuality equal and fair-minded. They are not, and they cannot be, for they are drawn from a community in which some are strong and some are weak. The strong impose their will but they do not do it in the public interest, except when that is also in their interest. Things work the other way round. The strong take pains to present what is in their interest as if it were in the public interest. The best that can then happen for any collectivity is that the strong fall out among themselves. Societies everywhere, large and small, have this problem, which is, of course, another aspect of the tension between the individual and the collectivity. All these features will appear as the narrative unfolds.

The sirdar, a taciturn, monosyllabic man, certainly no orator, usually had his point of view presented to a meeting by one of his henchmen. At the meeting held in the evening of March 19 he did, however, make the opening announcements. These concerned Ramnobomi. The performances commemorating Sri Ramchandro's life were staged in several places, some down by the river, another (the spectacular conclusion in which Ravana's palace was burned) in the harvested fields to the north of the village near the upper primary school, but most of it in Warrior street. The enactments were highlights in a continuous performance of reading aloud the text of the *Ramayana*. The place for this recitation—they gabbled most of it faster than commercials on American radio—was the forecourt of Sri Ramchandro's temple, which lay on the northern side of Warrior street. Each year they erected anew a temporary structure in front of the temple to protect the reciters from the sun, and they built a low wall around to discourage dogs, chickens, cows, goats, and children from straying into the hallowed place. (The temple itself was being reconstructed, a long business, and each year they repaired and refurbished a temporary structure that stood on the site.) None of this work had yet been completed, and the sirdar opened the meeting by announcing that it was imperative that every house provide one person to come and share in the task. He also said that a roster of those who came would be kept, and that should put an end to all the quarreling about who did the work and who shirked. (The threat seemed to be effective. I went to look next morning and there were about forty men present, a few working, and the rest watching them work.)

The sirdar had an abrupt almost military style of talking in public, and, besides, he was usually careful to avoid involving himself in arguments, preferring to come in at the end to announce what he had decided was the consensus. Consequently, when there was something controversial to be said, something that required diplomacy and a smooth tongue, he left the play to other people, no doubt priming them beforehand. On this occasion a Distiller, Sripati Pradhan, whom everyone knew to be an eager client of the sirdar, pointed out (no doubt in a tone of eminent reasonableness: I was not present that night, but I heard him on other occasions playing the persuader) that Monday was the day when the "work" (that is, the Ramnobomi rites) must begin. As everyone knew, he said, the community must be in an auspicious state at that time. But there had been a death the previous night, and if the normal mourning period of six days were to be observed, many households in the village would still be in a state of ritual impurity on Monday (March 23, only five days after the death), a situation that was highly undesirable. If they observed six days of mourning, they would be holding a sraddha on the day the Ramnobomi rites began, which would be very inauspicious. He offered a solution. He pointed out that the girl had not gone in marriage and therefore, he suggested, they could get the sraddha done within three days, and thus minimize the risk of having things go wrong.

Susila's father belonged to Jodu's faction. In the normal course of events all that faction (about ten houses) would have been maximally disabled. The sirdar's faction would also have been in mourning. They would have made a contribution, household by household, to the sraddha and have received food, but would not themselves have attended, and there would have been no need for them to enlist the services of a jati puo to cook for them. (The positions are the reverse of those at Kola's sraddha.) I have no record of how Jodu's faction reacted at the time to the suggestion that Susila should, in effect, be deemed to have been an infant, nor did I ask whether her father was at the meeting. Nor do I have any account of the sraddha. I have a later note that four of the five houses in Syamo's courtyard mourned for six days, and therefore disqualified themselves from the first day of the Ramnobomi ritual. (One household had some time earlier transferred its allegiance to the sirdar's faction.) Jodu's household stayed with them, also observing six days of mourning. The remaining five houses in that faction, like all those in the sirdar's faction, decided that three days would be enough. I have no doubt, conventions in Bisipara being what they were, they would have found it more difficult to bend six days into three if the near-adult who died had been male.

These gaps in my notes are understandable because the people who gave me an account of what went on at the meeting focused their attention (and therefore mine) on other matters. These other matters may also have been sufficient reason for the two factions not to have gone to the mat over the question of how long the period of mourning for Susila should be. The consensus was that Bisipara had a rogue devata on its hands and that something should be done about it at once.

3

Devatas

The March 19 meeting that arranged for the work on Sri Ram-chandro's temple and debated how long to mourn for Susila seemed to take it as a fact that a devata was loose in the village; her death proved it. So they decided to hire a gunia to find out whose devata was doing the damage and get rid of it. At this stage there was no open talk, so far as I know, about penalties or restitution; only about what they should do to remove the danger that hung over the community.

The decision was not disputed, nor was the diagnosis. The carpenter, when we stood outside the sickroom, had insisted that Susila's illness was just that, an illness and not a case of possession. But I did not hear a voice of disbelief again until the affair had almost reached its conclusion. Nor did the issue get itself snared in factionalism. Jodu's party (Susila's father being one of them) might have made the running, since they were the immediate sufferers. But both Jodu and the sirdar together came to ask me to take her to the hospital, which suggests it was not a partisan affair; on this they had a consensus, which they often did not.

That being so, I could not at first make sense of a resolution agreed upon at the meeting, because it seemed to anticipate dissension. The panchayat resolved that everyone must sign (or make their mark on) a document consenting to a divination.

The young man in the center, with a thread across his shoulder, is Bala, the younger of the two Brahmin brothers. All the others are Warriors. Madhia Behera is second from left in the front row. Debohari stands on the right. The older man next to him is the sirdar.

"That way," the sirdar said, "we won't have cases on our hands." I remarked on this and was rewarded with a cautionary tale. Somewhere over on the Kohenjaro side, Jaya said—he did not know just where—they held a divination and the devata got loose and possessed a man who seized an axe and killed three people. Evidently divination could be dangerous. Perhaps the village, by getting everyone's permission, was trying to insure itself against litigation. Kopilo had a more mundane explanation along the same lines. The investigating specialists would be going into house compounds, sometimes even rooms, and a litigious household might take the panchayat to court for trespass.

But that did not make much sense. Villagers, as I knew by then and they themselves certainly knew, were hypercautious about entangling themselves in the judiciary. There was nothing libertarian in this attitude, no sense that government institutions in themselves were evil. The problem was with the people who ran the judiciary; they could not be trusted to do what was right. There were a few officials—most of them remembered from the past—who, people said, were just and honest men. But for most of those who worked in and around the courts, the villagers had a healthy disrespect. Petition writers, pleaders, clerks, and the attendant policemen were all considered corruptible. Worse, the familiar device of a "gift" to a clerk to get a file moving was not enough; civil litigation was a three-way contest between the two litigants and the judicial officers (with their hangers-on) over the price of a verdict. Even witnesses had to be bribed. Why, then, if people were known to be so wary of the courts, should the panchayat see a need for a document signed to release it from possible litigation?

The answer reveals a curious combination of rationality and irrationality, which is certainly not peculiar to people in Bisipara. They knew it was stupid for a villager to go to court to sue another villager. The suit, even if won, would cost more than might be got in damages. A poorer plaintiff would likely lose. A richer one could find less risky and less expensive ways to get what he wanted. So a rational person would not go to court. But, as everyone knew, people are not always rational; they may not count the cost. Take someone to court, and you may ruin him, but at the cost of ruining yourself. People can do that, and in Bisipara they knew (as we do) that law courts may be used less to seek a settlement than to continue a war. Therefore, while it is irrational to litigate, it may be rational to *threaten* to do so, because your opponent does not know whether you are foolhardy enough to actually do it. The threat sets up a position from which to bargain.

The panchayat, as I made clear, has trouble implementing its decisions, judicial as well as administrative. Usually it negotiated with those it found guilty to get them to acknowledge responsibility and agree on a penalty. The situation is not unlike plea bargaining in American courts; the legal system's own deficiencies put a bargaining counter in the hands of the accused. It should be clear now why the Bisipara panchayat had everyone sign that document. It was anticipating threats to go to court and hoping to cut them off at the source. The panchayat often tried to protect itself in this way, producing a document that they hoped would constitute a constraining reality. Sometimes litigants were asked to agree beforehand (in writing) to pay a specified fine (the standard figure was twenty-five rupees), if they appealed to government courts against the panchayat's verdict. Sometimes the panchayat did not ask for signatures but simply threatened to "boycott" the offender.

The judiciary surely would regard such devices as void from the outset; no government court could allow a village panchayat to neutralize a citizen's legal rights. The villagers probably knew this; I never asked. I think they, half knowingly, were bluffing themselves, pretending that an alien legal procedure, the written agreement, would somehow let them freeload on the sanctioning authority that lay with the government. The government had what the panchayat lacked; police and prisons. The panchayat did seem unsure of the stratagem, because it often required those who might be tempted to litigate also to take an oath at the temple. Then the divinity, functioning as a peremptory amicus curiae, would punish those who broke their promise.

When the carpenter insisted that this was sickness and not possession, I did not think to ask how he knew that. What test did he use to determine there was no devata? For me it was different; the notion of possession (in my thinking, a neurotic affliction) never occurred to me. I just knew that Susila was very ill, and I know—although I did not think about it then—that a blood test would likely have shown what kind of illness she had. I also know with absolute certainty that no blood test (or any other scientific procedure) would have revealed the presence or absence of a devata in Susila's body.

But possession is an objectively real condition. In Susila's case it was agonizingly visible. Her body went rigid and then thrashed about, her eyes rolled back, her teeth were grinding: there are massive and unmistakable bodily indications of what they call possession. But to go further and name a possessing spirit as the cause was a poetic fantasy that had nothing to do with the medical condition of the girl. The carpenter was right, I thought, and those who talked about devatas were mistaken; they had the wrong answer.

To come to that conclusion, as I did (virtually without reflection) in the midst of the crisis, was to do the villagers an injustice. The fact is I had the wrong question. (I did not think much about it at the time; reflections mostly came later in encounters with notes and picking the brains of Romesh or Jaya or Kopilo or other patient people.) The question they were asking was not my question. In my scenario, Susila had the bad luck to be bitten by a mosquito and contract malaria. It would never have occurred to me that there was any use in asking *why* it had happened. Nor would it have made any *practical* sense to me to ask who was to blame. Of course that is not a foolish question. I could have said it was her own fault for not sleeping under a mosquito net or not taking Paludrine; that line would have led back to a series of culpabilities, ending probably with the government for not having a better health service or a better malaria eradication program. But thoughts like that would have seemed quite irrelevant, when faced on March 18 with the problem of what could be done to save the girl. The cause of her sickness, in that sense of "cause," was her bad luck, or an act of God, or fate; by definition, there was nothing to be done about any of them.

What I had missed was that the two explanations that the carpenter made into alternatives—"This is not possession; it is a sickness"—were not, in the Bisipara way of thinking, mutually exclusive. Susila was sick; and her sickness was the result of possession. The implication, of course, unlike explanations from luck or God's will or the inexcusable incompetence of government, was that something could be done about the problem then and there: steps could be taken to remove the possession. (I assume they did so; that would account for the presence in the compound of the Potter, who was a gunia. If he did try his hand, he failed, and that may be the reason why they sent for me.) Does his remark imply that the carpenter did not see the world in the same way as other people in Bisipara? Probably not, for he made no protest later when they were planning the divination. I think he only wanted to convince them that the drugs I had or those the hospital might provide were worth at least a try. He was a pragmatic man.

Possession by a devata is only one of many ways to explain illness in Bisipara, some of them as commonsensically empirical as our folk beliefs. Cold weather, for example, brings on fever. (They are right about the timing, of course, but I never heard anyone blame the mosquitoes and the water lying around at that time of the year.) Too much exposure to direct sunlight, they believe, gives you a headache. Indeed it does; and they are careful always to shade their heads when they are outside. When the nauseous jackfruits ripen and children gorge themselves, they get a bellyache. In the hot weather the mangoes begin to fall from the trees, and fruit flies breed in them. Fruit flies have a liking for the human eye, and small children (adults too, sometimes) get conjunctivitis. People try to protect themselves and their children by applying a thick dark eye shadow. There was also a wealth of folk wisdom about what to eat and what to avoid when sick or when pregnant. People were given to worrying about regularity, for they consumed, by our standards, vast quantities of rice at a sitting, and all that bulk food required at least two, preferably three, expeditions a day to keep healthy. (I recall giving Jodu the postmaster's second son enough laxative to move a mountain, only later discovering that his persistent requests for aid referred to the day's *third* visit to the fields.)

Sickness that lingered or was obviously serious evoked a different kind of explanation, one that made a single category of bodily ailments and other kinds of misfortune. If a man's cow drowned in the river, or his house burned down, or he had a really bad deal trading for turmeric, or he had more accidents in the forest than is to be expected—cut himself with an axe or speared his foot on a sharp bamboo—or was injured by a wild animal or bitten by a snake, or he or someone in his family suffered from a continuing illness, then "his planets [horoscope] have gone rotten." Bisipara people used the same word, *khorap* (rotten), to refer to fruit gone bad or to a person with a marked character defect or to a horoscope that indicated misfortune. Kola, whose sraddha I described earlier, had his planets go rotten. First his ox died. Then he himself fell down a gully (he was an old man). His wife's sari caught alight when she was squatting by the cooking fire. Then he died. There was, Jaya told me, another disaster surely on the way for Mithu, the heir, unless he did something about it. He would have to bring in a Brahmin, who would read his horoscope and make a *puja* (a rite of worship) to set things in order.

Susila's house had not, so far as I know, run through a series of misfortunes of that kind, but they did bring in the headmaster to read her horoscope. I do not know what he told them. In any case, an inauspicious positioning of the planets would not have ruled out other more immediate causes for her sickness. Possession seemed the obvious cause; it was clearly indicated by the symptoms. Enthusiasm, in the root sense of being possessed by a divine force, was familiar enough in Bisipara. That condition, which is sometimes referred to as "altered states of consciousness," the villagers saw as a feature of the body more than of the mind. Susila's violent and uncontrolled movements were in the same category as the behavior of men or women who went into trances. Both were evidence of being seized by a devata. Possession also was manifested in the occasional convulsions and frequent episodes of craziness that afflicted Ganesa, a young Brahmin priest who, I was told, probably had tertiary syphilis. The central feature in all these instances was the seizure, bodily movements not under the control of the person making them.

Other evidence emerged, or was invented, even by the time of the meeting, the same day that Susila's body came back to the village and was burned. The story of the little Herdsman boy who died suddenly in the night expanded to meet the new situation.

He died on February 28, and I wrote a note about it the same day. He died in the night, Romesh said, and no one knew why he died. But by the time they came to talk about Susila's death and to decide whether they should hold a divination, the story of the Herdsman boy had been elaborated. He had been heard to cry out, in his sleep, the name of the Washerman's little daughter, Bijuli. There was not a word of this in the original account. Perhaps he did; it may not have seemed significant then. At that time they were not looking diligently for causes, probably because the boy, although not an infant, was not yet beyond the age when, as they see it in Bisipara, the hold on life is still tenuous. Deaths of small children are distressing, but not unexpected.

The Washerman and his family lived in the compound adjoining that of the three Herdsman brothers. The Washerman's wife attended when the women took the dead child's mother down to the river. The Herdsman boy and the youngest son of the Washerman had been playmates. The two households were at the western end of Warrior street, on the southern side, neither of them as grandly constructed as the solid central block of Warrior compounds. The Washerman (the Oriya word is *dhoba*) followed his trade, and, like the two Barber households, a Brahmin household, a Herdsman, and Chanti, the Sweeper woman, was a servant of the village. The institution that regulated their service is called *jajmani*. Each household of clean caste is a *jajman*, the person who engages a *kamin*, the one who does the work. When paddy is harvested and threshed, the kamin receives a fixed share of the grain (still unhusked, as *dhano* or paddy). Each time he performs the service for his jajman's household, he receives a quantity of husked rice (*caulo*). Lowly people, like Chanti the Sweeper, are given cooked rice (bhato), and every day at noon she would send a child around with a big dish to collect it from each of her jajman houses.

These people—Brahmin, Barber, Washerman, Sweeper—do a job. Market rules apply, somewhat. Kamins are hired and fired, but supposedly not for economic reasons. Bisipara's senior Brahmin, Oruno, for instance, had fallen foul of the leading Warriors (both factions; his political skills were not good), and the panchayat dismissed him and appointed his younger brother, Bala. The younger brother was inexperienced, and I attended several rituals at which the elder brother squatted by his side and prompted him, from time to time breaking into an impassioned plea for his position (the word he used translates as "privilege") to be restored to him. The Washerman too had his problems with the big men of the village, as you will see. For a kamin, bad work (or treading on the wrong toes) could mean the sack.

But in other respects a jajmani relationship is more than economic, more than just an exchange of services for payment. First, it is a marker of status; only the clean castes can command the services of a kamin. Untouchables, no matter how rich (a few were rich) cannot. Second, other kamins besides the Brahmin provide essential *ritual* services. No marriage, no funeral rite, no betrothal can be done without the assistance also of a Washerman and a Barber.

The head of the Bisipara Washerman household was called Debachano Behera, nicknamed Tuta. *Tuta* means "broken" or "crippled"; he walked with a slight limp, the residue, possibly, of infantile paralysis. He had four sons and four daughters, two of them married and gone to their husbands' villages. Two sons were grown and able to take on work, but not yet married. The youngest boy was the playmate of the Herdsman child that died. Tuta was prosperous, having, with the help of his sons, a clientele both in Bisipara and in Gonjagura, across the river. Out walking, I would see the family, three men and sometimes the wife and one of the daughters, down at the river, thumping clothes on the rocks and spreading them out to dry. Tuta cultivated some land as a sharecropper and (it was said) did a little money lending on the side. He lent out paddy at interest to households that ran short before the harvest came in. He traded in the market at Phulbani, intercepting peasants as they arrived, buying their produce, and reselling it at a profit. (I heard later than he had been fined for operating with a rigged scale, my informant remarking that he must have been too mean to pay the right sweetener to the inspector.) Two weeks after we came to the village he arrived at the bungalow one morning and sold us peanuts that he had grown. One of his sons took land in a sharecropping arrangement, and all his older children, if they had nothing else to do, hired themselves out as day laborers. The family did not lack in energy or enterprise. But they lived without ostentation, giving no outward signs of wealth. People knew, nevertheless, that Tuta's household was not one that went hungry.

It was also rumored that Susila cried out in her delirium "The Washerman is consuming me!" She may have done so; but by the time I saw her she was beyond speaking. Nor did I hear of this accusation until after the villagers were launched into their witch-hunt, which is what the affair became. Susila's dramatic seizures were sign enough that she was being possessed by a devata. Now, the story went, they had direct evidence that the offending devata belonged to the Washerman; Susila herself had said so. There was also the revised version of how the Herdsman child had died. Devatas on the loose, the reasoning went, go after young people, not old ones, and both the young people who died lived near the Washerman's house. If the Herdsman boy had cried out "Bijuli!", the name of the Washerman's little daughter, that was one more piece of circumstantial evidence that Tuta's devata was the one that had run amok.

Devata means "deity," and in general refers to all divinities. But the context of Susila's death and the witch-hunt gives the word a narrower span. In that context devatas are spirits located in particular places, attached to, and "kept" by individuals. I found it hard at first to grasp what people envisaged in the word devata. Nevertheless, following my penchant for intellectual order and consistency, I tried to pin the concept down.

Ghosts (bhutos) and ancestral spirits (*pidera*) were not devatas. Some divinities, although devatas in a general sense, were regarded as belonging to a higher order and were not in the same category as the devata that possessed Susila. Shiva and Vishnu and their various incarnations qualified for this elevated status. Those divinities were openly and publicly worshipped by their devotees. They also sometimes possessed people, putting them in a trance. They could do good things for a person or the community. They were not, however, devatas like the one kept by Tuta.

Devatas of that variety are versions of Devi, the wife of Shiva. Durga and Kali, for instance, are manifestations of the Devi's dark side. Others, such as Parvati the mountain goddess, represent Devi's benign aspect. To worship these divinities is not necessarily to "keep" them. Durga, under the name of Mongala, the auspicious one, was worshipped in several houses in a night-long ritual in October. The rite was most elaborately (and most expensively) done by those who had promised to sacrifice a goat if Mongala granted a wish (usually recovery from illness). Smaller desires required offerings less costly than a goat. If the wish was not granted, there was no sacrifice. Ekadosi Bisoi, Syamo's elder brother's son, made such a vow to save his daughter's life, but the child died anyway, and so he made no offering. The concluding part of the rite ensures that Mongala, having been feted for that one night, is removed from the premises. A cotton wick is lighted in a leaf cup of cooking oil and floated away down the river.

The devata that Tuta kept turned out to be Durga, whom he had installed in his compound. The verb is *rokhiba,* which is used like our verbs to "place" or to "install" or to "keep." Debohari "kept" (habitually used) a "blade," the English word they use for a safety razor. A woman "places" the cooking pot on the fire. A husband "installs" and "keeps" a wife. He does not "install" his children; but he does "install" an adopted child or a live-in servant. The notion seems to be that of setting up a stable arrangement in the context of doing something useful. In Tuta's house Durga was a year-round fixture.

Devatas, like many divinities, were both one and many. A shrine near Pano street, tended by a Pano priest, was dedicated to Thakurani (the "lady" or "princess," the deity of smallpox). Thakurani, propitiated in an annual ritual, could also possess people, both those who got sick and others such as her priest. No one, so far as I know, kept Thakurani as a personal devata. The shrine at the back of the mandap, with its relics, was the seat of a devata, Komeswari, the guardian spirit of the Warrior lineage in Bisipara, and therefore of the village itself since the Warriors were (or had been) its lords. One member of the Bisoi lineage, a man living in the new settlement to the north of the village, was Komeswari's priest, and I saw him conduct the annual ceremony for her at the end of May. I have no record of her possessing people.

Other deities that watched over communities were the objects of private devotion. One such was Bhuani, a central player in the drama that is to follow. She lived, apparently ubiquitously, in rocks and streams and trees around the village. She was a benevolent and helpful spirit and was, so to speak, the devata of choice for Bisipara's diviners. It was Bhuani whose aid the diviners enlisted to identify the devata that had caused Susila's death. Without Bhuani's help, they could not uncover the cause of misfortune and recommend a remedy. Bhuani seemed to be a semipublic divinity, one nurtured by particular persons but also available to serve the public interest.

Some devatas, although ubiquitous, at the same time inhered in particular places, and if you owned the place you had to care for the resident devata. Debohari took me out to a field in late June that year to watch him propitiate its resident devata. The rains had come, and he had plowed the field and was about to broadcast paddy seed. He took a chicken to the corner of the field (a very small chicken), made a little heap of rice, threw some turmeric powder over it, mumbled something, had the chicken peck at the rice, cut off its head and sprayed the blood over the rice heap. I asked him why he did it. He said if he didn't do it he would get a bad crop; that is, he corrected himself, he might get a bad crop; or something bad might happen. Anyway, the chicken was cheap. There would be no sense in running a risk by not making the offering. I had the impression that Debohari put the sacrifice in the same techno-economic category as the improved seed and the chemical fertilizer he sometimes got from the government's farm extension service at subsidized prices. It might or might not work, but it cost so little anyway. Debohari was a schoolmaster, rational and clear-headed, perhaps the man who most educated me about Bisipara and its ways.

Oruno, the Brahmin who had been sacked from village service, also had a devata. He got it (the name I heard was Push-padurga, Durga of the flowers) from his mother-in-law; he was by no means keen to have it, but the devata more or less installed itself, making its presence clear by a few small mishaps that befell Oruno. Then he knew he had to propitiate it. A devata in one of the houses in Potter street removed itself to another house, its new owner being made aware of his responsibilities in the same way that Oruno had been. At other times people talked of devatas almost as if they were commodities: a deal could be made with someone who had a devata and was willing to part with it. One man in Bisipara, a Potter and a gunia, kept two devatas: Parvati and Bhuani. Oruno the Brahmin and the unwitting Potter were the only two men, in my records, who took on a devata reluctantly. Every other instance was a deliberate choice.

Keeping a devata, except in the case of the gunias, was not unlike the discreet keeping of a mistress. (They did that too, sometimes a widow—recall Kopilo's adventure with the widow Rua—or a servant girl or, less often, someone's wife taken in adultery.) There were differences. Discretion had a lower threshold for devata. One did not boast about having a devata, but, if it became known, normally it would not be denied. The practice, as will become clear, skirted the edges of ethically correct behavior, but it was not in itself unambiguously immoral. Concealment, in fact, was not easy because devatas were kept on or near the premises, being installed in a tree in the garden, or a fence post, or a wooden pillar or a stone built into the wall of the cowshed or the house. There was no effigy or icon to be seen, but there were always telltale signs of offerings made: a few grains of rice (soon cleaned up by ants, wild birds, chickens, or one of the few household dogs) and, longer lasting, the stains of turmeric powder, red ocher, or blood. Courtyards and gardens were private places, but not entirely closed to the neighbors' eyes. Sooner or later someone would see the householder doing what I watched

Debohari do in his paddy field. In the case of gunias, of course, everyone knew that they kept and propitiated a devata; otherwise they could not have done their job as diviners.

Gunias were rewarded for their services, especially when they were able to get things back to normal. The rewards were far from substantial, two or three rupees, a little more than twice what a laborer was paid for a day's work. Their motivation, I guess, lay somewhere between disinterested service to the community, ministering to their own prestige, and practicing a skill.

Those who kept devatas and were not gunias got a different kind of reward, more indirect, more uncertain, and distinctly more material. People kept devatas because the devatas brought them luck. Luck, in this case, was quite narrowly interpreted to mean material prosperity. The man who went out to Kond villages to buy turmeric and sell to a merchant in Bisipara or Phulbani might make a small offering to his devata before he set out, and another more generous one if he made a killing on the deal. Good harvests or success in commerce, especially when one's neighbors were not faring so well, were evidence that the devata was doing its job.

Wealth, in Bisipara's philosophy, came in two ways. There were some men, for example Jodu the postmaster, who worked hard, were skilled cultivators and careful managers of their farms, and who invested wisely in cattle or land when the opportunity arose. They were solid, shrewd, respectable, and responsible men of property. That kind of wealth carried with it the suggestion of the-world-in-its-place, part of the order of things, of dharma, and therefore was right and proper. Without exception in Bisipara legitimate wealth was (in 1953, it may be different now) connected with owning land, with respectability, with hierarchy, with permanence and stability. It was long-lasting slowly accumulated wealth that stretched down the years—rational wealth, so to speak, that came from careful planning and accrued only to those socially entitled to be wealthy. Almost by definition, this was inherited wealth. Tacitly, also, such wealth belonged in the domain of maleness, the central core of order and stability in the community.

The other kind of wealth reversed this image; it was a fluke. It was the kind of wealth that goes with the idea of a lottery, of rewards that are undeserved, that come out of cheating, of individualistic and opportunistic behavior, or, at best, out of plain luck—what we might call "the Devil's luck." Jodu inherited the estate that he managed so well. But Jodu's father, who had built it up, worked as foreman of a post office maintenance gang in Phulbani, and he made his fortune, people said, by inflating the salary sheets and cheating the workers. Distillers, like Basu Pradhan's father and grandfather, had become rich by cheating Konds. Another man (Chano Mehera, who will appear later) found a pot full of gold coins—so people said—when digging foundations to extend his house. Such wealth was easy, unearned, undeserved, and by implication antisocial, a threat to dharma. It is entirely consistent that Durga and Kali, manifestations of femaleness, of both creative energy and destructiveness, should be agents for those who prospered in that way. Women, the creators, are also the destroyers. Such sentiments were tacit, not voiced as philosophical truths; they were built into the taken-for-granted image that Bisipara people had of their world and its patterning.

Easy wealth, people said, was the primary motive for deliberately installing a devata in the homestead. That was also the reason why those who inherited a devata, like the one Debohari had in his paddy field, were careful to service it. If they did not, the devata might remove itself to a better place (as in the case of the one in Potter street), taking prosperity along with it. Alternatively, it might turn vicious ("hot" was their word) and inflict misfortune on a negligent guardian or, indeed, at random.

Keeping a devata was an ethically marginal enterprise not only because easy money has a dubious status, but also because devatas can harm other people. Durga, the source of energy and prosperity, is a destroyer. Tuta's devata, people eventually decided, took possession of Susila and killed her. They used the word *khorap* (rotten) for that kind of conduct; the word indicates, in the devata as in the planets, something that has become actively harmful.

Our logic indicates that the person who kept the devata should bear responsibility for the damage it does. But Bisipara's moral judgment hesitated at the margin. The situation was that of the farmer whose bull escapes from a field and gores an innocent passerby, or the owner of a dog, hitherto docile, that suddenly turns vicious and bites a neighbor's child. The argument can go many ways. This was an act of God, it may be said. Or it was an act of God helped out by the farmer's scandalous failure to maintain his fences. Or it is in the nature of dogs to bite people, but no one can tell when they will do so, and, in any case, many people keep dogs that never do harm. A similar menu of moral judgments is available when a devata goes on the loose. Even then the mere keeping of a devata is not ipso facto an act of infamy. Except in the case of the gunia, however, keeping a devata can easily be construed as antisocial.

Some men, who (I think, but am not sure) do not enter this story, used devatas as weapons to attack other people; they were like sorcerers. Their work could be detected, and sometimes countered, by a gunia. The several stories of this kind that I heard were all, except one, about Konds. The exception, a text written by Jaya two years after the events described here, identified Tuta the Washerman as just such a sorcerer. People feared to let small children play near Tuta's house, Jaya wrote. But Tuta also doubled as a curer. When people fell sick, they could send for Tuta, because they knew he was so powerful. If he refused to come, that told them he was the one sending the sickness. This story looks like a tradition invented after the troubles of 1953, because it is hard to believe that a reputation so unambiguously evil would not have been immediately bandied about at the time of Susila's death. Feelings so powerful should have made themselves evident the instant the witch-hunt began. But I am not sure, for it was the case that out of several possible victims Tuta did become the principal quarry hunted down in 1953.

When a man kept a devata and things went wrong in his own house, he might decide that the fault lay with the devata, not with himself. Despite the care he had provided, the devata had become "hot," and worse would happen to him if he did not take action. These decisions might be made for him by a gunia, aided in the diagnosis by his own devata. There was a complex power relationship directly between devatas; in particular, good devatas could be used to track down wicked ones. Strong devatas, unless properly propitiated, might inhibit the actions of other devatas, even preventing them from coming forward when invited by their owners.

If a man feared that his devata was becoming a danger to him (or, I suppose, to other people), he might expel it. A later chapter will describe how this was done collectively for all the bad devatas in Bisipara. I have no record of how individuals did this in Bisipara, but I have some notes on the procedure in Kond villages. Konds in contact with Oriya villages such as Bisipara (as they have been for several centuries) had much the same repertoire of devatas. Indeed Bhuani was Kond and was usually addressed in the Kond language (Kui). Oriya was also used, since Bhuani, like most of the men (but not women) in villages around Bisipara, was bilingual. But the Konds also had another type of devata, with the same tutelary-make-me-rich function. These devatas were physically represented by small brass statues, made by the lost-wax process. Some are (or were) on display in the Victoria and Albert museum in London. I have a few: a peacock, several representations of oxen, complete with plowman, yoke and plow, several that look like cauldrons, with the remnants of offerings still stuck inside them, a soldier, and a man brandishing a sword and holding a hookah (water pipe) in the other hand. I have also seen representations of cobras. Even in 1953 these statuettes were hard to find. The explanation that I was given for scarcity was that, life in the Kond hills being very harsh, more and more people concluded that their devatas (in Kui called *penu*, plural *penga*) were overheating. The owners cooled them by throwing them into the river. So they became rare and have since become museum pieces.

This cognitive domain (the world of the devata), as it appears in my notebooks, is far from orderly. The categories run into one another, and the domain spans two distinct but not separated cultures, represented by distinct languages, Kui and Oriya, the former belonging to the Dravidian family of south India and Oriya being Sanskritic and therefore an Indo-Aryan language. Moreover, as the story unfolds further, it will become clear that several people had an interest in undermining one version of truth (about how things were done and how they should have been done) and making another version stick. Nevertheless, I think I see certain general features in this categorical imbroglio, and a statement of them will help to make the events that are to be described later seem less bizarre.

The heart of the matter is a tension between certainty and uncertainty. We pin things down intellectually—we escape chaos—by making intellectual models that identify patterns of events and, beyond the patterns, their causes. These models let us recognize what has happened, tell us what is the appropriate action, and even sometimes allow us to shape future events—at least to plan to do so. Sudden fever and convulsions were modeled by me (helped out by the civil surgeon) as cerebral malaria. Most people in Bisipara modeled the same events as possession by a devata. Each of these models both explains past and present events and suggests appropriate action, both immediate and in the future. They are, to use Ibsen's splendid phrase again, the "lies that make life possible."

They are lies only in the sense that they are, each in themselves, incomplete explanations of experience. Each explanation leaves a great deal unsaid. Each of the two models answers a different question, and if you use one to answer the other's question, you get a bad result. The possession model codes in a cure, but not directly; it allows you to infer that the possession must be removed. But the model is, in the medical model's universe, a lie, because the procedures that purport to remove possession will have no effect on malaria. The medical model, in its turn, has nothing useful to say about the other model's main question: *Who* is responsible for Susila's sickness and death? The medical model, in fact, is fundamentally different from the possession model because it is scientific; the possession model has to do with morality.

Both models summarize or contain within themselves a way of looking at the world, which is different in each case. The medical model is the model of science; nonhuman, one might say, in the sense that it looks for regularities that are predictable because the causal connections that operate within the model do not depend on someone's whim, or on their perception of right and wrong, or on their self-respect, or on any other human characteristic. The practice of medicine and the attitudes people have toward diseases do raise moral considerations at every turn, but the etiology of a fever does not. The causal links that connect still water with the breeding anopheles mosquito, which conveyed *Plasmodium falaparum* into the bloodstream of the girl, and all the other connections in her body that eventually led to the destruction of her brain, operate without any deliberate human intervention. They are events in nature, not subject to human choice, and therefore not open to moral judgment. The model is a model of *things*, automatically linked, machinelike. As such, it gives the illusion of certainty, of being accurately in correspondence with an objective world. (It is an illusion because the real world is always vastly more complicated than the model, and such models work only when "other things are held equal.")

The possession model is quite different. The certainty it envisages is not in the hard objective predictable world of nature (as our culture, but not Bisipara's, claims nature to be); it is a moral condition toward which everyone should strive. It is not a model about things, but about *persons*. It is not about events, but about actions. It is not about what happens but about what *should* happen and what people *choose* to make happen. If they make choices, they bear responsibility. They open themselves to ethical judgments about good conduct and bad conduct, innocence and guilt. Tuta kept a devata. He chose to do so, and to that extent he was responsible for the consequences. How far he should be held responsible inevitably became a matter for argument, a question that could never be settled so objectively that everyone would have had to agree on a verdict. A blood test would have shown what particular strain of *Plasmodium* killed Susila. Such a test would be objective precisely because those who accept its verdict also agree upon the conditions that separate a valid from an invalid result. In the domain of morality ultimately the same considerations apply. The difference is that moral antagonists are usually unwilling to agree upon what will constitute a valid test, with the result that there are no "objective tests"; there are only opinions and unending arguments both about ultimate values and about what conduct is or is not in accordance with those values.

Susila's case emerged and escalated rapidly into an acrimonious dispute (in Oriya called a *golmal*) because in some respects it contradicted expectations contained in normal models. Sixteen-year-olds should not get sick and die in that fashion. Nor is it normal for anyone to get that kind of fever when the hot weather is so far advanced. If Susila had been a year old and died in December, that would have saddened those who knew her, but it would not have made them anxious and angry. If, at her age and in the middle of March she had developed the other common Bisipara affliction, one or another form of dysentery, the thought of possession would most likely not have crossed their minds. Some other explanatory model would have been invoked. The following year an adolescent boy with epilepsy took a fit and drowned face down in a paddy field. No one talked of possession or devatas on that occasion; it was just the kind of accident that people know can befall an epileptic. The problem with Susila's death arose because the wrong thing happened to the wrong person at the wrong time of the year. "Wrong" in this context has no immediate moral reference; it does not indicate wickedness. It simply means that a pattern of expectation had been disrupted.

When that happens with a scientific model, the scientists are supposed to busy themselves with improving and correcting the model. (It is well known that they often are reluctant to do so.) The other kind of model, a moral system, can question itself only with great difficulty, if it can do so at all. In fact these models contain within them the equivalent of self-sealing or fail-safe devices, which provide those who fear to question fundamental beliefs or values with explanations for what has gone wrong. The particular devices that I have in mind at present—there are many other kinds, including the habit of refusing to recognize inconsistencies—take the following form: The model is fine but people are wicked or stupid. The social order is beyond question; if things have gone wrong that is because people did not follow the rules. For example, they kept devatas that ran amok. If Tuta had not kept a devata, Susila would not have died.

That explanation is perfectly clear, and it is the one that eventually prevailed in Bisipara. Tuta denied his guilt; and so did the four others who were accused along with him. But they did not reject the model of the way their world worked. Yes, they agreed, it was the case that devatas could escape and do harm; it was not the case, however, that *their* particular devata had consumed Susila. Undoubtedly the order of things had been disrupted; but they were not the disrupters.

There is another level of explanation, another and more fundamental way in which an expected normality had been disrupted. From an outsider's perspective (mine, eventually), Tuta's devata was a metaphorical expression for Tuta's disruption of a moral order. Tuta, in other words, had crossed some line that Washermen should not cross.

That kind of disruption will come to the surface later. The next step is to describe the diagnostic procedures that the villagers followed to identify the source of their troubles.

4

Bhuani's Search

Nothing was said, when the panchayat met on March 19 to arrange a divination, about Tuta's devata being the killer. They conducted themselves, as civilized people do everywhere, with an ostentatious (and somewhat hypocritical) concern for due process. Inquiries, they seemed to insist, should follow proper procedures and issues should not be prejudged. First the facts should be ascertained. Only then could one proceed to consider questions of guilt. But it was common knowledge that Tuta was to blame. It would have been a nine days' wonder if the divination had revealed that Tuta had no devata, and a very big surprise if the verdict had been that his devata had done no damage. But in those early days Tuta's guilt was kept as an open secret.

The procedures they were about to initiate were not primarily accusatory. They were intended to cure a collective illness; the analogy is not with a prosecutor, but with a healer. The proclaimed purpose of the operation was to remove evil forces from the community, not to penalize those responsible for the evil. This attitude, which probably did not represent the community's true feelings, was quite in accordance with the way it handled its own litigation; the ostensible goal was always to restore harmony, not to punish.

The procedure they followed was, in a way, scientific. They could have gone about the work quite differently, more or less as

I did when I asked Jaya or Kopilo or Debohari how one knows that someone is keeping a devata. They could have produced witnesses to say they had seen Tuta make offerings by the jackfruit tree in his garden. They could have examined the tree for traces of past offerings. They could have produced more circumstantial evidence, pointing out that Tuta (or other offenders) seemed to be inexplicably prosperous, when everyone else was having a hard time. But to encourage tattletales is obviously not a way to bring harmony to a community, and so they followed a different procedure. Of course, some conflict was inevitable: uncovering Bisipara's equivalent of a pact with the Devil could not help but stir up passions. If, however, it could be done impersonally, apparently without human intervention, those judged guilty might be resentful but they could not so easily claim that the decision was prejudiced. The verdict would, so to speak, be externalized; neither the community nor any person in it would bear responsibility. By their very nature places like Bisipara have trouble with situations that require impartiality. From there issues the warrant of the panchayat itself; it speaks with the voice of the Divinity who stands above them all.

The embodiment of objectivity in this case was a man bearing the title of *dehuri*, which I will gloss as "priest." *Dehuri* is a lineage name, found in several castes. It is also a title given to those who serve a "public" devata, for example Komeswari or Thakurani in Bisipara. The dehuri imported to conduct the divination in Bisipara came from Dangolu, a village four miles south of Bisipara along the Salki river. He was a Warrior, and he brought an assistant (an Oilman) and a couple of other men, both Warriors. On Thursday night they decided to invite him; they sent a delegation to Dangolu on Friday; and he arrived in Bisipara early on Saturday morning, March 21. The walk from Dangolu takes a little over an hour, and the visitors reached Bisipara before the sun had come to its full heat. (By noon that day the shade temperature on our veranda was 105°F.) The matter was arranged more briskly than was usually the case in Bisipara, where faction rivalry and the norm of consensus together were apt to make public business move slowly, when it moved at all. On this occasion they found a quick consensus, in part because they were under pressure to cleanse the village and have it in good spiritual order before the Ramnobomi rituals began the following Monday.

All priests, by virtue of their work, stand at the margins of a community or, perhaps, above it. They are sacred; they represent the portion of every person that belongs to the collectivity—to the body, as it is said in New Testament Christianity. The sacred is the part of us that is shaped by the community's beliefs and values, in other words, our conscience. Likewise, gunias and dehuris, while they are on the job, themselves become part divinities, embodiments of the collectivity. Therefore they are supposedly impartial, impersonal, and endowed with the kind of authoritative neutrality that we attribute to science. (The man from Dangolu was doubly impartial since he did not belong to Bisipara or any of its factions.)

The dehuri and his party came into the sirdar's courtyard and were given tea and tobacco. (This is dried but uncured tobacco leaf, shredded and smoked in a rolled green leaf. The mixture is quite harsh, and a few puffs are usually enough to satisfy the smoker.) Meanwhile, in the street outside, the materials and personnel needed for the ritual were being assembled.

The central feature of the rite is a charpoy, the wood-frame-and-string bed. *Charpoy* has the suggestion, missing from the English word *bed*, of "throne" or "seat of honor." Few houses have more than one or two of these, and most people sleep on a mat on the floor. The charpoy is locally made from the wood of the *sal*, hard as oak and as heavy. The long and short stretchers, about sixty and thirty inches respectively, two of each, are let into the legs by mortice and tenon joints, and pinned with bamboo plugs. No nails or screws are used. Nails are expensive and are rarely employed in carpentry because sal wood splits unless holes are first bored to receive them, in which case bamboo is just as effective and virtually costless and does not rust. Woodscrews are unknown; nor is glue ever used in woodworking, because none known to the village craftsmen was proof against the extreme humidity of the monsoon season. Joints in a new charpoy are firm and tight, but one wet season followed by the desiccative heat of summer is always enough to make them loose. All charpoys are rickety, but, being held by the bamboo pins and braced by the cords woven across the stretchers, they do not fall apart. In the gaps left in the joints and the space under and between the cords, live colonies of bed bugs. Every village charpoy is infested. To accept a seat on a charpoy (proper etiquette dictates that it be offered a visitor of high status) is to offer oneself to the bugs.

The charpoy used on this occasion came from Potter street, from the house of one of the gunias. It was brought first, without ceremony, to the street outside the sirdar's house. Then four young men carried it to the river, bathed it, and brought it back to Warrior street. A bath is a ritual act, a preparation for doing sacred things. Men and women bathe before eating a meal or taking part in worship. In just the same way the charpoy was bathed to make it ready to receive the devata who would be invited to occupy it (in this case the benevolent Bhuani). The four young men were the charpoy's bearers, their task being to carry it on its journeys around the village. They each held one leg in the palm of an upturned hand. The work proved exhausting as the heat mounted, and relays of handlers succeeded one another, succumbing to violent headaches (which were attributed to the proximity of the devata) or to a blistered hand. The sirdar had selected the first set of bearers from among those who were strong enough and unmarried. (Some were married—all but a few marriages are arranged—but the wives were not yet mature enough to have joined them in Bisipara.) Many rituals, including this one, require the principal actors to have been celibate for a stated period before the rite is performed. This condition, they believed, could more easily be met by those who did not have wives. Old men might have qualified, but they were considered not strong enough to carry the charpoy around the village.

The dehuri accompanied the charpoy to the river and supervised its further preparation in Warrior street. A stretch of ground had been swept and prepared with a plaster of mud and cow dung. When dry, it made a smooth clean surface. On this the charpoy was placed. Pieces of cloth were wrapped, like scarves, around the middle of the four stretchers, and small brass bells were tied to the legs. Two more substantial lengths of new cloth were tied across the head and the foot, as vestments for the devata. Then the dehuri made offerings to the spirit of the earth and the spirit of the mountain. When they had been propitiated, he made the third and crucial offering that constituted an invitation to Bhuani, the devata that was to do the work, to install herself in the charpoy. The offering consisted of *lia* (unhusked paddy prepared as popcorn is made and loosely molded into forms, with molasses as the binding agent) and a libation of *modu*, a colorless liquor distilled (illegally) from the flowers of the *mahua* tree. Lia features in many Hindu rites; it is also a respectable refreshment to offer honored guests. Liquor has no part in local Brahminic observances. But it is found in every Kond ritual. (A skilled Kond officiant can pour a libation the size of a pinhead. Making modu is a lot of work.) The dehuri, on this occasion, was not a Kond but an Oriya Warrior. When he first arrived and was exchanging politenesses with the sirdar and others, he spoke Oriya. He addressed the earth spirit (*Tana penu*) and the mountain spirit (*Soru penu*) in the Kui language; Tana penu and Soru penu are not part of the Hindu pantheon.

The words of his invocations (which were by no means brief) were lost on me. I did not understand the Kui language, and the prayers were gabbled at high speed, the esoteric style making it clear that the content of the message was not addressed to the bystanders but to the devata. (Later, when I looked into these matters and took down invocations in writing, it became clear that the object was to leave no spirits out of the listing lest they take umbrage and block the rite's efficacy. A Kui invocation to ancestors, for example, ended with the words "and anyone I forgot.")

Kui language apart, I could not have understood the dehuri's words because I could not in fact hear them. The rite was accompanied by some very loud and obtrusively rhythmical music.

Important occasions and important people are, in Bisipara as else-where, celebrated with music. On this occasion it was provided by a huge drum, slung from the player's waist and shoulders and adorned with stag horns, by two other drums that resemble our side drum, by a tambourine (without the jingling disks) two feet in diameter and played with a stick, and a man playing the shrill oboelike instrument that in the Kondmals they call a *mohuri*.

The musicians stood a few yards away, just inside the semi-circle of spectators, most of whom, along with the band, had escorted the charpoy to the river. The musicians were untouch-ables. The oboe player was the husband of Chanti (the Sweeper woman who worked for us), and the drummers were Panos who lived in two courtyards off the track to the southwest of the village, well away from the main Pano street, which lay to the northeast. When the dehuri was coming near to the end of his preparatory ritual, a woman came out of the sirdar's house with a large platter of lia and some other foodstuffs and laid it on the ground close to the senior member of the Pano household, who was present but not playing an instrument. He picked it up and carried it away. (That is the way things are exchanged between clean-caste people and untouchables; direct contact is avoided. Romesh, buying eggs that Panos brought to the bungalow, would either have them put straight into a bowl of water—if they float they are bad—or hold out his hands to catch the egg dropped into them by the Pano.)

I recognized several men from the main Pano street, the one to northeast, including the senior village watchman, the sirdar's lackey. He was wearing his official turban and the sash with a badge of office and was carrying his staff. The Pano men around him were fidgeting, almost dancing, to the rhythm. One of them was unmistakably tipsy. Then one man (not the drunk) came forward and, quite insistently, took over the big drum, at once thumping out a louder and more compelling rhythm and, sud-denly, contriving to turn a spectacular cartwheel—drum, horns, and all. One by one the other players were relieved of their in-struments, or, in the case of Chanti's husband, replaced by a man

Musicians. They are untouchables. The oboe-player is Chanti's husband,
a Sweeper. The others are Gumsur Panos.

who had brought along his own oboe. The music seemed to take
on a professional quality that it had lacked before. I had seen the
same thing happen two weeks earlier, at Jaya's wedding.

The Panos from the old street to the northeast were the village's traditional musicians. It was their "privilege" to provide
music on festive occasions, at village rituals, or in households at

Gumsur Pano musicians.

weddings or betrothals. For this service they would be paid a small amount of money, and they were entitled to sit down at the feast, in a line apart from the clean castes, and be given a share of the cooked food. Some time before I came to live in Bisipara the Pano musicians had got above themselves (according to Jaya), demanding more money and sitting down to be fed even when they were not themselves the music-makers. The whole caste, Jaya indicated, was forgetting its place, being encouraged by politicians and social workers and recent legislation to demand entry into temples hitherto barred to them. So the panchayat appointed others in their place. The replacements came from a much smaller group of Panos, a more amenable lot, who lived on the other side of the village, and from Chanti's household. Unfortunately their skills did not approach those of the musicians who had been dismissed.

Individual Pano households were linked to Warriors in a jajmani-like arrangement. But it had a different name, *raja-praja*, king-subject. Each Warrior household stood as king to one or more Pano households, its subjects. The Panos were farm laborers. They received a share of the harvest; in addition, the person working would each day collect cooked food from the master's house. Ideally the relationship continued down the generations, and a praja was less an employee than a retainer, an appendant of the master's household. On festive occasions the praja received a gift of new clothing. The praja gave his services, as needed, for weddings and funerals and other ritual occasions in the master's household, and the master made appropriate gifts for the same occasions in the praja's house. The idiom of total responsibility and total service was much more developed in Bisipara than in our present-day society. I could provide a job description for a praja, because people could tell me more or less what a praja did. So, in our culture, I could tell you what a mother or a brother or a son does, but the phrase "job description" would surely seem out of line. The verb in "what a son does" is the lesser consideration; what matters is what a son "is." That was the way people in Bisipara thought of raja-praja. Their idiom was feudal, familial, noncontractual; unquestioning service and mutual loyalty were (supposedly) the norm. The relationship was not evaluated against money; it was a relationship, a matter of conscience, not a series of transactions.

But by 1953 the raja-praja relationship had become almost defunct. There remained only two such links still active, both involving a sirdar household. In both cases the head of the praja household was paid a small stipend by the government to assist the sirdar in his duties. One of Bisipara's watchmen was the sirdar's praja. The bureaucracy, in other words, was helping inadvertently to preserve a small remnant of feudalism.

The presence of two different groups of Panos in the village (there were occasional intermarriages) reflects its history. The village was founded several hundred years back—there are no written records—by Oriyas who came up into the hills from the small Hindu kingdoms on the plains below. (The tax-defaulting raja, whose misfortunes led the British into the Kond hills, ruled one such kingdom, lying to the south of the hills, toward the coast

and the Bay of Bengal.) Bisipara's tradition was that they themselves had come from the north, from a kingdom called Boad
in the valley of the Mahanadi river. The settler group were Warriors, the original "owners" of the village, together with their
serving castes, who were Herdsmen, Brahmins, Distillers, Barbers, Washermen, Panos, and a few others. When, in the nineteenth century, the British took control of the hills, they came
up from the coastal region, from the south and east, and they
brought coastal people with them. Others came in their wake,
as modest opportunities to make a living in trade or in government service opened up in the Kond hills. The newcomers included Distillers, Brahmins, Herdsmen, one or two other castes,
and Panos. Such castes are distinguished in Bisipara by pref-
acing their name with "Gumsur," the name of a kingdom lying
south of the hills. Thus Bisipara contains Boad Panos and Gumsur
Panos, Boad Herdsmen and Gumsur Herdsmen, Boad Distillers
and Gumsur Distillers, and so forth. Boad and Gumsur people
of the same caste sometimes marry. But such marriages are reckoned risky, in accordance with the strong feelings in Bisipara that
only like should marry like and that the other lot are surely inferior, if not unsavory. Moreover, as the Boad-originated castes
saw things, Gumsur people, even after a century, were still im-
migrants, at best peripheral members of the moral community,
in some lingering way a threat to the dharma.

When he had propitiated the earth spirit and the mountain
spirit and had invited Bhuani to occupy the charpoy, the dehuri
carried out a test to see if everything was in order. Thinking about
it later, I imaged the procedure as a pendulum that swung between mystical fantasy and quite hard-headed empiricism. One
process, which conjured up a fantasized entity, which no one
had ever seen and no one presumed to describe (they could describe a bhuto, a ghost, quite clearly), was followed by a perfectly
objective test, binary in form—either it is the case or it is not
the case.

That was my image, not theirs. I sort out the natural from the
supernatural; they did not. Against this, it might be argued that

the "fantasized entity" (the axiom of a devata as an explanatory force) is conceptually not so very distant from the postulated forces of natural science (such as gravitation), but to imagine they were reasoning in that framework is, I think, mistaken. They thought in terms of social rather than natural connections between entities. I think they saw the entire procedure as an exercise in persuasive manipulation, likely to be effective so long as correctly done. The aim was to construct an opportunity context such that any rational devata would have no choice but to do what the dehuri "requested" it to do. In a way they were thinking like the economists and political scientists who design policies on the premise of rational choice; the essence of the procedure is to construct the right incentive structure. Alternatively, the devata could be like a computer that has to be programmed the right way. But machine analogies are not part of Bisipara's thought patterns. Devatas are like people, not like machines. Computers, despite appearances, do not make choices in defiance of their programmers; devatas, however, may do just that. Therefore everything has to be as right as possible so as not to give the devata an excuse for not cooperating.

The test was to have me hide a four-anna coin (a quarter of a rupee), and send the charpoy to find it. If it failed, they would know that Bhuani had not installed herself. I went off, accompanied by Jaya, feeling like an actor pushed on the stage without being told his lines. I was quite sure that the charpoy had no means of knowing where I hid the coin, that the search would be a fiasco unless rigged, and that Jaya had been sent with me so that one way or another he might give the handlers a few clues about where to look. My skepticism must have been transparent (I said nothing), because Jaya, as soon as we were out of sight of the crowd in Warrior street, stopped, turned his back, and told me to walk on and hide the coin. I deduced that Jaya intended the test to be genuine. But my skepticism prevailed, and I walked only a few steps forward, hid the coin beside a garden fence, and rejoined him. In that way, I thought, he must know within a few yards where it was hidden. In fact Jaya was not a skeptic; he wanted the charpoy to prove itself or be disqualified.

The charpoy set off, accompanied by the musicians and a gaggle of onlookers, to find the coin. As the day wore on and the heat intensified, most of the spectators abandoned the charpoy when it went any place where they could not find shade. The musicians were reduced to a single, increasingly lethargic, drummer. But at this first stage, still in and around Warrior street and the compound where the bungalow lay, the charpoy and its handlers were attended by an obviously fascinated throng of people, among them (quite unusual) a cluster of married women. The handlers included, in addition to the four youths carrying the charpoy, the dehuri's assistant (the Oilman). Sometimes the Oilman put questions to Bhuani; sometimes other people did.

The charpoy, its four feet held in four independent hands, took on the natural swinging motion that goes with walking. When it came to a place where a devata might reside, the questioner faced the charpoy and spoke to it, addressing it usually as "Ama!", the Kui term for "mother," occasionally by the equivalent Oriya word "Ma!" (The nurturant qualities that we construe in *female*, are not necessarily connoted by this usage. Gender in the Kui language puts males in an exalted category, and everything else in a single subordinate category: women and girls, animals, birds, insects, gods and godlings, and inanimate things.) When the handlers were standing still, the swinging motion continued, but gently. The questioner would then ask if a devata was present in this place. If the motion continued unchanged, still gentle, that showed there was no devata. If the swing became more violent—when it did, the questioner sometimes had to put up a hand to protect his face—a devata was present. The questioner then continued, putting the names of different devatas to the charpoy, until the quality of its movement indicated that he had submitted the correct name. Then came the crucial questions: Was this a harmful devata? If so, was it responsible for the recent deaths? Whatever the answers, the householder or some other responsible person was expected to mumble some words of respect and throw a small offering of uncooked rice over the charpoy, which would then go on its way.

Bhuani visited the devatas that were, so to speak, in the public domain, paying her respects to the village temple (Ramchandro's abode), to the mandap devata, and to various other places, including the large Shiva temple situated on the edge of the village, a hundred yards from where I lived. On these occasions no questions were put. The charpoy was allowed to swing enthusiastically for a short time and then someone, the keeper of the shrine or the sirdar or, out in the fields, whatever important person was in attendance, would throw rice over it so that it could continue its rounds.

The behavior of the charpoy and the people around it brought home to me, even on that same day, the peculiar melding of inside and outside that occurs in the domain of the sacred. On the one hand Bhuani conducted herself as a person of high status in the community and was herself accorded the appropriate etiquette. For example, she paid a visit to an old man who lived on the north side of Warrior street and was himself the sirdar of a neighboring district (he was also the nominal head of the faction led by the postmaster). He was very old, crippled with arthritis, and stammered badly, but he emerged from his house to say something (in Oriya) and to throw rice over the charpoy. The Bisipara sirdar also was visited by Bhuani, and, early in the day, accompanied the charpoy on its rounds, sometimes putting questions to it (in Kui). Our cookhouse, which stood thirty yards away from the bungalow, also had a visit. The cook, an old Herdsman who came from Phulbani, was volubly annoyed at the intrusion; but he did throw the required handful of rice, somehow managing to underline the dismissive element in that gesture. At the other end of the social scale, Bhuani visited Pano street, where no person of high status would normally go. On this occasion some of them did. Being sacred, she was outside and above the normal restrictions that protect high status, and her presence presumably gave immunity to the clean-caste people who accompanied her into Pano street.

Some of this externality derives from the fact that Bisipara people, although they knew that Bhuani is a manifestation of Devi, somehow see her as belonging with the Kond pantheon.

The name itself, I assume, must be a version of Bhawani, one of the many names carried by Devi, Shiva's wife in her milder form. Bisipara people do not indulge in classificatory exercises to construct a logical ordering of their myriad divinities, and I never heard Bhuani's ethnic affiliation debated. The Konds have an elaborate cult of the earth spirit (Tana penu), and for a time, doing what Bisipara people do not do, I tried to tidy up the situation and categorized Bhuani as the Bisipara version of the same deity. (*Bhumi* is the Oriya word for what Konds call *tana*, the earth.) But no one said this, and later I recalled that the Kond deity was separately propitiated (under its own name) at the time Bhuani was being installed. On the other hand almost all direct communication with Bhuani was carried on in Kui, although all the interlocutors (mainly the dehuri, his assistant, and the sirdar) had Oriya as their first language. (There were in fact only four or five Kond households in Bisipara, all of them recently arrived, the men seeking jobs as farm laborers. Across a stream to the west and south of the village was an old Kond settlement, containing four households.) Bhuani, moreover, seemed, in certain ways, insensitive to Oriya ideas about caste pollution.

In the Kondmals, the subdivision in which Bisipara lies, five in every eight people were Konds. The term *ethnic* was not in vogue in 1953 as it is now. It lay still within the domain of anthropology as a somewhat technical alternative adjectival form of "tribe" or "race." But its present-day connotations of prejudice, strife, and fundamental and ineradicable difference suit the history of Kond-Oriya relationships quite well. The history began, as I briefly outlined earlier, an unknown number of centuries back, when Oriyas from the neighboring lowland kingdoms migrated into the hills. Whether they came as marauders, conquerors, or fugitives or were sent to serve as Lords of the Marches, or some mixture of these capacities, I do not know. What is clear, looking at the distribution of Oriya villages on the map, is that they settled in the broader valleys where irrigated rice fields can be constructed. Cultivation outside these areas is done by slash-and-burn techniques. The Oriyas lived in fortified settlements, and there are tales that tell of the part they played in wars between Kond clans. Very likely they participated in the rite of human sacrifice. In March 1846 a military detachment under Lieutenant MacPherson was intimidated into releasing back to a mob of Konds some of the potential victims, whom they had taken under their protection. This event took place at Bisipara. It is clear, however, that the Oriyas were in no sense a conquering elite.

The Meriah Wars brought an end to this balance of power, if that is what it was. The conquering British understood the Oriya language; they did not understand Kui. Oriya speakers became the agents of the imperial power and were able during the second half of the nineteenth century and most of this century's first half to dominate and exploit the Konds. By 1870 the main police post for the area was established at Bisipara. Power was no longer derived from weapons of war in the hands of every man, but eventually fell to those who had forensic skills, the capacity to use the law to deprive others of their land and their wealth. A particularly bad episode came about 1880, when missionary intolerance combined with administrative greed to ban home-distilled liquor. Its sale continued through licensed outlets. The licenses were purchased by Oriya Distillers, who sold liquor against a mark put by illiterate Kond landowners on documents that transferred property to the shop owner. Gumsur Distillers became, and remained in 1953, the largest per capita landowners in the village; Boad Distillers, in per capita holdings, were equal to the Warriors. The administration eventually realized what it had done; all drink shops were closed in 1908, and various measures were taken to put an end to this and other forms of exploitation. But the language barrier and illiteracy (Kui is not a written language) ensured that the Konds have remained for most of this century an underprivileged and often exploited majority.

The Oriyas who first came up from the plains brought with them the caste system. Bisipara people stereotype one another according to caste and ethnicity. For example, Konds consider all Oriyas, especially Panos, potential exploiters. Oriyas, Warriors in particular, regard Konds with a mixture of paternalistic affec-

A Weaver's household. The wife of Daiteri Mehera's son readying cotton thread for a shuttle. There is a charpoy in the background.

tion and contempt, judging them to be simpletons, too honest for their own good. Also—a cause of great hilarity in Bisipara—Konds consider cow's milk disgusting and polluting. The Oriya legend is that they taught the Konds how to grow rice and even taught them to wear clothes. Before they knew better, Konds wandered naked in the jungle. Derogatory stereotypes are also held by Oriyas about each other. Warriors think of Distillers in the way that aristocrats anywhere think of the newly rich: pretentious, tricky, and without honor. A Pano myth tells how the Warriors of Bisipara made no headway in a war with the Konds of Domosinghi until two brave Pano heroes came to their rescue. Other castes say that Panos are thieves—administrative records show that officials shared this belief—and people pointed to the

A Gonjagura Potter.

fact that Panos had come to own all the land around their own street. Former owners sold out to Panos, the story was, because Panos invariably stole the ripening crops; thieves make the best watchmen, especially when they watch their own property.

Each caste has its distinctive place in the dharma—Warriors as landholders, Panos as their subjects and workers on the land, Brahmins as their priests, Barbers, Washermen, Herdsmen, Fishermen, Oilpressers, Basketmakers, Distillers, and the rest—each performing an allotted task and all joined into a single work-integrated community. In the modern sense of the word, however, such a community is not integrated at all. Certainly there is no idea of equal opportunity. The level at which persons are born is the level at which they should stay, and the different levels are marked and reinforced by everyday interaction. Castes are made distinct by elaborate customs that have to do with relative purity (untouchables at the bottom and Brahmins at the top), a separation conclusively marked by food and by marriage. Cooked food is a potent conveyor of pollution and may pass only between equals or from the pure to the less pure. To accept these foods from someone of a different caste is to acknowledge one's own inferior status. To refuse it is to claim a higher status. The other marker is marriage. All proper marriages take place within a caste; therefore all kin are within one caste and all caste-fellows are actual or potential relatives.

There has been much academic dispute about what governs the ranking system that makes one caste high and another low, but one fact is abundantly clear. A caste that has become rich, as in the case of the Bisipara Distillers, does not easily accommodate itself to a low place in the ranking system. Likewise, when members of a low-ranking caste become well off, those of high rank, particularly if they are themselves not prospering, will do whatever they can to put the upstarts back in their place.

Oriya opinion is ambivalent about where Konds fit into the caste system. Warriors accept water from a Kond, as they do from their own Herdsmen, but not from Barbers, Washermen, Distillers (the Distillers respond by not taking water from Warriors) and certainly not from their own Panos. Warriors would refuse food cooked by a Kond; some Konds accept it from Warriors and some do not. There is thus a measure of ambiguity about food and the status of Konds. There was, however, in the 1950s, no uncertainty about marriage: Konds should marry Konds and no one else. But this constraint cannot always have been the case. The Potters in Bisipara claim they are the descendents of the union of a Potter man with a Kond woman, and there are similar groups in many Oriya villages. The adjective *sito* (I think it is an abbreviated form of a word meaning refined or educated) is applied to castes of pure descent; *kondho* to those of mixed descent. The Bisipara group are Kond Potters; those in Gonjagura are sito Potters. A similar distinction is found among Herdsmen, Smiths, and Panos, but not, so far as I know, in any other caste. Finally, to complete this pasticcio, I was told (in a tone of someone letting the skeleton fall out of the cupboard), "We Warriors are nothing but Konds who became rulers."

There is a pleasing irony—a sophistication if it were conscious —about using the tar-brush of one's own ancestry as a device to create the qualities of sacredness, externality, and impartiality. Bisipara, unambiguously Oriya in its own estimation, uses a divinity that belongs, somewhat ambiguously, to the inferior Kui culture, gives the divinity an Oriya name, addresses it in the inferior Kui language, and elevates it to the realm of the sacred; not to speak of treating it with the same forms of respect that it uses for nondivine persons of consequence such as the sirdar, myself, policemen, and officials. The categories, as I said, flow into one another and, as the full complexity becomes apparent, it is quite hard to discern, under the wash of Kond cultural influence, dubious ancestry, an influx of alien Oriyas from the south and of alien ideas from the bureaucracy and the government, and an almost universal readiness to seek personal advantage from those ideas, the pristine social order that the community seemed so anxious to preserve from violation.

The initial foray of the charpoy took it to the houses of the two sirdars, the mandap, the temple, the cowshed behind the Bisipara sirdar's house, Tuta's house (where it lingered for quite a time), the house of a gunia in Potter street, then inside the bungalow where we lived, then into our cookhouse, then to the house of the poor Christian widow, which was nearby (I had concealed the four-anna piece in the fence around her garden, where it may still be), and then back to the village. It came again later, just before midday, interesting itself in the shed where my van was parked. By that time I had gone inside and I heard the sound of loud and heated argument, which, Jaya later explained to me, was caused by Bhuani herself. Bhuani was getting hot, not in our sense of being close to finding the coin, but in the Bisipara sense of being bad-tempered and dangerous. So they took her down to the river and gave her a bath to cool her off. I noticed also that from time to time, later in the day when they were making the rounds, someone would come out with a pot of water and throw it over the charpoy. The four young men doused themselves in the same way; they were hot too.

The quarreling broke out because Bhuani had failed the first test; or, as they put it, she could not have entered the charpoy. If she had, the coin would have been found. They went ahead anyway, and only later—when the quarreling started—took steps to set matters right. There was a man in the village at the time, an agent for a company that collected *kendu* leaves, which are used to wrap the *bidi* type of cigarette. (The leaves are collected from the forest in the hot weather. A gatherer in 1953 was paid one pie—twelve pies to an anna—for thirty leaves, which would mean nearly six thousand leaves to earn a rupee. The accounts for one day at the Bisipara shed show thirty-five collectors, payments ranging from two to six annas. Most of the collectors were women and girls.) The village touched the bidi agent for a rupee. A Warrior man took it and hid it, and this time Bhuani found it. By now the shadows were at their shortest, and the handlers parked the charpoy in the place where they had first consecrated it, and everyone went away to bathe and eat a noonday snack and have a sleep.

Bhuani failed to find the coin that I had hidden. At the time I did not ask why they thought she failed, and nothing more was said about it on that day. The divination began again later in the afternoon and continued into the evening in an atmosphere that, toward the end, seemed quite buoyant, a mingling of excited anticipation with the satisfaction of watching work well done. I assumed that Bhuani had saved the situation by finding the second coin. The next time I heard the matter mentioned was the following Thursday. The village was already three days into the Ramnobomi ceremonies, and the evenings and nights were filled with pleasurable activity that occupied the front stage of public affairs. Behind the scenes, however, the devata affair continued to unravel. There had been some complications, to which I will come later, arising out of the Bhuani rite. I listened to some men who were sitting around talking about the work done on

March 21. Obviously things had gone wrong, one man said; if they had been done properly there wouldn't be all this confusion. The charpoy failed to find the coin (the one I had hidden); that was proof enough that Bhuani had not been properly installed; the whole thing should have been called off there and then. His listeners seemed to agree.

Recalling my behavior and my thoughts at the time, I realize that I was waiting for them—even wanting them—to reveal that they were as unbelieving as I was myself. I was ready for Jaya to tell me where to hide the coin and then see him go back and somehow pass the word. Precisely that procedure, I was quite sure, had been followed when they hid the second coin. I was not disturbed if old men and old women, or small children, were taken in by these poetic fabrications; nor was I put out by true-believer behavior from people like gunias who had a clear vested interest in the system. But I wanted people like Kopilo or Romesh or Debohari, rational clear-headed persons who were making it their business to educate me in the culture of Bisipara, to stand back and externalize that culture in an objective and scientific manner.

That feeling was—and still is—second nature for me. I recall the sense of embarrassment, almost consternation, when in the course of an oral examination of a doctoral candidate studying a religious sect in California it became clear that he accepted, as a literal observable empirically verified fact, the capacity of the sect's guru to levitate. How could one conduct a rational discussion with someone who believed such things? Did he not realize that levitation was a metaphor that symbolized spiritual freedom from bodily entanglement? Presumably, I thought uncharitably, he would see nothing strange in taking a ruler to measure the tail on Maxwell's Demon.

But my science was not theirs. The nearest they seemed to come to my way of seeing the world was a mild and occasional skepticism. A month later I talked to Kopilo about the hand that destiny had in shaping his life. In 1935 a son, ten days old, had developed a rash and a fever. Kopilo got some herbal medicine from the present sirdar's father, but it did not help, and people urged him to call a gunia. He did so, and the gunia (a Kond) said that a devata was consuming the child and the best course would be to promise an offering to Mongala if the child recovered. He himself didn't believe much in devata, said Kopilo, but there was nothing to lose. In fact it cost him nothing, because his son died soon after. (This was the attitude that I saw also in Debohari, sacrificing a chicken in his field.) Kopilo, nevertheless, was not so skeptical about other things. Ten years earlier his mother had died. He called in a Brahmin who diagnosed a severe fault in the family's astrological condition revealed by comparing the dates of the mother's birth and her death. He advised Kopilo to leave his house for at least four months. Kopilo moved his wife and the child Romesh to Phulbani, where he was teaching at that time, leaving the house in Bisipara to be guarded by a caretaker, an elderly Warrior who had a reputation for being unusually honest.

The man whom I heard say the ceremony should have been called off as soon as Bhuani failed to find my coin was another such person. Sindhu, a Pano schoolmaster, judicious, calm, and articulate. He was also a devotee of Shiva and officiated each week in a temple he had constructed in Pano street. On this occasion, the Bhuani ritual, here they were, all of them, taking the procedure at face value, treating the coin-finding test as a scientific experiment that would determine objectively whether or not a metaphysical entity had demonstrated its nonmetaphysical existence. I did not realize at the time how unreasonable my expectations were. Kopilo and Romesh and the others were not thinking in terms of metaphysics. They believed in the instrumental reality of Bhuani. Bhuani, if the proper arrangements were made, could get things done just as Basu Pradhan or myself or the civil surgeon could get things done at the government hospital in Phulbani. Failure would not have meant that Basu and I were metaphysical constructs; failure meant that arrangements had somewhere gone wrong or, possibly, someone was being bloody-minded. I was, I see now, no less imprisoned in my own way of thinking than they were in theirs.

Later I was offered, indirectly, an explanation for the failure to find the coin. On Saturday, April 11, another divination was held, and from the outset it was clear to everyone that the devata was not being cooperative. After some discussion I was asked to stand farther away. Devatas, I was told, are often shy about presenting themselves before people of high status. By extension, I suppose, they might be reluctant to go in search of a coin hidden by such a person. I suspect that the speaker was being diplomatic and that my status (*bara sahib:* important person) was less the issue than my status as a nonbeliever. That line of thought came out unambiguously in a story Debohari told me about a subdivisional officer who was attacked by a bhuto when spending the night in an inspection bungalow, similar to the one in which we lived. He was going out of his mind, Debohari said, and would have died if a gunia from the village had not come to save him. I asked if that could happen to me. Not possible, Debohari said, because he knew I did not believe in ghosts. "If you don't believe in them, how can they hurt you?" The logic of this is a world in two parts, an inside that is the community of believers, and an outside where beliefs and values are different. What surprised me— but perhaps is apposite—is the suggestion in the metaphor that the forces that keep the inside world in motion, for good or for evil, are ineffective beyond its boundaries. But the reverse is not the case; the potency of my unbelief seemingly could influence the behavior of devatas. (The further conclusion to be drawn— depressing for an anthropologist, but hardly unexpected—is that I was truly an outsider.)

I still have several unanswered questions about what went on that day. Bhuani was said to select her own route around the village and its environs, periodically deciding on a visit to the river to cool down. Some of the day I went along, and, mapping those parts of the journey that I followed, I could find no pattern. The movements seemed to be random, going from one street to another, doubling back, going outside the village, then returning, then venturing out into the fields again. The obvious rational procedure is to move systematically, as with a mine detector, up one side of the street and down the other, and then move on to another street. But that course was not followed. The only regular move was the periodical trip to the river.

When the charpoy moved, carried by the four youths, it went ahead, and the assistant, or whoever was acting as questioner, followed behind, with the musicians and the crowd behind him. There was no discussion that I heard, not even suggestions, about where to go next. It is, of course, possible that the entire performance had been rehearsed, that the youths knew where they had to go to uncover devatas, and that they had been told to do so in a random fashion, drawing a lot of blanks (which they did) to make it look convincing. But that seems unlikely; the heat took its toll, and there were frequent and apparently unplanned changes of bearers in the course of the day. (Some of them, if I remember correctly, were young married men whose wives had already come to join them in Bisipara. Bisipara people are not, to say it again, overly finicky about the details of procedures they insist they must and always do follow.) Perhaps, then, the entire village was into rigging the test? But that made no sense. Who would then be left to be deceived?

Nor did I ever make much sense of how the movement of the charpoy was regulated. A gentle slow swinging indicated no devata present. When another devata was encountered Bhuani caused a swift and violent movement. Given the way the charpoy was balanced in the palm of the hand, any one person of the four could easily influence the length and strength of the swing. Therefore only one of them need be in the know about where to find and where not to find devatas. But the idea that they colluded beforehand in determining where and when devatas would be detected does not make much sense. It would work for encounters with known public devatas (those located in temples and shrines), or known gunias, or notorious people like Tuta. But this was the day that they discovered the devata in Potter street which had shifted residence, a fact, they said, that had not been known before. Maybe that was a plausibility stratagem, too? It seemed unlikely. I was also reluctant to believe that adolescent males knew much about village affairs or that they would know where to go look. I was probably wrong on that; a huge amount of tacit common knowledge lay around in Bisipara.

Alternatively, there may have been some "Clever Hans" device whereby the questioner signaled the answer that he wanted from the handlers. I doubt it; in the course of the day they ran through a lot of handlers and a lot of questioners. The same thoughts are relevant, of course, to the crucial final questions: Was this particular devata harmful or not? If harmful, was it responsible for the deaths?

Five harmful devatas were uncovered. Oruno the Brahmin kept Pushpadurga. At the opposite end of Warrior street Tuta had installed Durga. In Potter street in the house of a man called Syamo Dehuri, Kali was found. In Hatopodera, Bisipara's market area, the spinster Srimati, said to be a Weaver by caste, kept a devata, for which I do not have a name. Last, in the new overflow settlement to the north of the village, Bagoboto Pradhan, a Distiller, kept a devata, that name also not being recorded. The three known names all belong to the Hindu pantheon and are manifestations of Devi, the wife of Shiva, in her malevolent form. All five devatas were harmful. Tuta's devata, the divination revealed, had possessed and destroyed Susila and the Herdsman boy.

CHAPTER

5

The Divination Completed

At dusk they brought the charpoy back to Warrior street. Later they held a meeting to decide what to do about Bhuani's discoveries. Normally they would have assembled in the mandap, but on this occasion they met in the sirdar's courtyard. They had no choice because the mandap was already crowded with visitors, men from other villages, early arrivals for the Ramnobomi festival. To air Bisipara's problems in front of them would have been embarrassing.

The opening ceremonies were due two days later on Monday, March 23, and on the Sunday there were still many things to do. Sri Ramchandro's birthday celebrations, being so near, had made them hurry through the witch-hunt much faster than they found comfortable. Susila's body was brought back to the village and cremated on Thursday. They organized the divination, with unaccustomed promptness, for Saturday. Later some people said they had been too much in a hurry, not because they held the divination that day, but because they persisted with it after the charpoy had failed to find the hidden coin. But all the people of the village (*ga loko samaste:* a phrase they often used to suggest a persuasive consensus, in the way that politicians here pontificate about "the American people") seemed anxious to get the matter tidied away as effectively and as soon as possible.

Partly they looked on the problem as one of contamination,

as we would think of hygiene; they wanted the place spiritually disinfected. They faced a gross incompatibility between the celebration of Sri Ramchandro's birthday and a funeral rite (Susila's sraddha). But that was not the main problem; they had already found a compromise over the sraddha. Mostly they worried about the surpassingly inauspicious presence in the village of malevolent devatas that had already demonstrated a tendency to run amok. Their religious concerns shaded into semilegal apprehensions of the kind that earlier prompted them to make everyone sign that quitclaim document. Bisipara would have many visitors over the next two weeks, and if any of them were seized by a devata the village would be in trouble. There were in Bisipara, as there are in many places, a few legalistic, risk-shy, superpessimistic people whose forward thinking was unremittingly negative and focused always on liabilities. The rest, normal people, I suspect were more worried about the village's good name— about what people might think and say than about what a devata might do to the visitors.

But, first and foremost, they felt a compelling need for the community to enter the two weeks of celebrating the birth of Sri Ramchandro in a state of peace and social harmony. It was the custom, the night before the first rituals, to hold a feast "in happiness" (khushi re), as they phrased it. In 1953 the sirdar and a man from Potter street each provided a goat. After darkness fell on Sunday, March 22, they went to the river, a mile south of the village (the Salki flows northward), to a big mango tree on the river's far bank and cooked a festive meal. Everyone went, they said. I did see a straggle of people setting off in that direction, but certainly not everyone—just those who would play active parts in the festival as reciters or players or musicians, together with some other men from the panchayat and the usual straggle of small children tagging along with a father or a big brother. Two goats go a long way, for Bisipara people eat meat in minuscule portions, more as a relish than a dish in itself, but two goats would hardly have fed the entire village.

Jaya and Romesh, talking to me about the "in happiness" feast, volunteered the reason for it. For the next two weeks no one should eat meat. (They rarely could afford to eat meat, anyway; they did so mainly on festive occasions.) Fish and onions and cooking oil pressed from seeds (such as mustard oil, or the mal-odorous stuff they extracted from the seeds of the ever-useful mahua tree) were also forbidden. Cooking should be done in *ghi* (clarified butter), which for most people meant Unilever's vege-table oil, Dalda, since ghi was very expensive. (Dalda came in a can and no one drew attention to its oilseed origin.) The common feature in all this is the taking of life, of the animal, or the fish, or the life that inheres in seeds and (they insisted as they do else-where in India) in an onion. Ramnobomi is a time to refrain from violence and killing. A deer or a wild boar or a peacock could walk through the street, Jaya explained (they were keen hunters); no one would harm it. So the night before abstinence they treated themselves to a small version of carnival, tasting meat one last time before they gave it up (for two weeks) to show respect for Sri Ramchandro.

I could not resist asking what would happen if someone broke the rules. I was rewarded with the tale of what, a year or two earlier, befell the father of Gopinath (Gopi) Dehuri. Alcohol also was forbidden during Ramnobomi. Most clean castes in Bisipara were not drinkers (except Kond Potters). Panos did tipple, and I often heard the din of drunken quarreling coming across the fields from their street. Konds drank. Walking in the forest I sometimes came across a little group of them around a toddy palm, at any stage of inebriation from talkative hail-fellow-well-met to flat on their backs. (The tree must be climbed to tap it. Falls and broken limbs sometimes ended such parties.) Gopi's father was a Kond Potter and a drinker. One evening he came to the festivities already drunk. During the night his wife died. Next day, realizing what he had done, he was so overcome with guilt that he too died. That shows, Jaya explained, that if you believe in the rule and break it, you will be punished. (It is the bhuto over again and the closed world of true-believers; if you are a nonbeliever, you cannot be harmed. Something in their collective experiences alerted them to the condition of externality and its potency. Certainly the alien world beyond their communities had proved, in the past century, to be unfriendly, unprincipled, and very powerful. The more common belief, encountered elsewhere, is that infidels are made vulnerable by their unbelieving.)

The meeting in the sirdar's courtyard, having been formally apprised of the results of the divination, imposed fines on the offenders. Four of them were to pay three rupees each. The fifth, Tuta the Washerman, was fined seven rupees, since his devata had done the damage. All the offenders were present at the meeting. So was Tuta's wife, a feistier person than her somewhat dismal husband, who limped about the village, even before the present troubles erupted, in a cowed and cringing fashion, as if all the world had it in for him. (His paranoia turned out to be justified.) Tuta's wife said plainly and positively that the divination was wrong; they did not have a devata, let alone one that had got loose. At first the men ignored her, as I saw them do a few weeks later when the wife of another culprit, Bagoboto Pradhan, started to speak her mind. On this occasion Tuta's wife, standing on the fringe of the crowd in the sirdar's courtyard, eventually got their attention, and a man answered her saying that Tuta, like everyone else, had signed the document agreeing to the divination, and he was therefore obliged to accept its verdict.

Tuta went home (fifty yards away) and came back with seven rupees. The others handed over their fines except Bagoboto, who said he was a poor man and could not afford more than two rupees. Would they accept that? The panchayat agreed, although everyone knew he was not that poor.

An adolescent girl died and a child died, and what went on the day the girl died made it abundantly clear that the community was deeply disturbed. Yet when they identified the person responsible for the two deaths, they fined him seven rupees. Other people who had been criminally negligent, at least as I saw it, had their negligence assessed at three rupees. Seven rupees was not a trifling sum. A male laborer, working a full day, at that time was paid one rupee. (A woman got a quarter less, twelve annas.)

Even so, the equation works out at two lives being valued at one week's pay for unskilled work. Obviously that cannot be the message of the seven rupees; my logic was surely not Bisipara's logic. Other things must have come into the reckoning.

I can think of several. Three weeks later, with little more information than was available on March 21, the panchayat raised Tuta's fine almost ninefold, to sixty rupees; and I saw him pay it, all of it, and I watched it being counted. One can deduce from their behavior that the panchayat members, Bagoboto's plea of poverty notwithstanding, knew very well that they were not, in those first fines, dipping very deeply into anyone's purse. Seven rupees and three rupees, if not quite token amounts, certainly were not disastrous for those being penalized. The round figure used in most of the panchayat's verdicts was twenty-five rupees (although they knew that culprits, having agreed to pay up, would in fact hand over no more than a fraction of that amount).

Since seven rupees and three rupees were not much more than token amounts, I reasoned, this fact must say something about the nature of the offense. I recall a faint feeling of satisfaction on discovering (as I mistakenly thought) that the panchayat was more rational (by my reckoning) than at first appeared. Evidently, I thought, like me they were working with a principle of partial responsibility. A good judge would want to be shown that the defendant was fully aware that what he was doing would cause harm. Tuta had not, as Kond sorcerers were said to do, deliberately sent his devata out to kill another person. The devata's escape was an accident. Tuta was still culpable, and should be punished, but not with the severity that would have been appropriate if he had been a deliberate killer. That was my reasoning.

But no one said that, and when I fished for agreement from Kopilo, I had the impression that he thought it an interesting and, in that situation, a quite novel way to regard the matter. They did talk about degrees of responsibility in Bisipara, but it was not the guiding idea on this occasion. The conversation with Kopilo went its own way, and I did not manage to ask him plainly why he thought the fines were so small. At the time the Ramnobomi festivities were going strong, and Kopilo spent most of his time with me explaining what the performances were about. When I came back to the devata affair, some days later, Tuta's case had become formidably more complicated.

There is a possibility, not unlikely, that two contradictory ideas coexisted in Bisipara minds. Everyone lives with contradictions; we do when we acknowledge that the same people can be both selfish and generous. Business is business and someone goes to the wall; other times we are our brothers' keepers. Their thinking about devatas could have been like that, the emphasis at any particular time going either way.

For example it is part of human nature (to use our idiom) to keep a devata and try to get rich, getting ahead of other people. Everyone does it, if given a chance, and there is nothing sinister about wanting to be rich. Sometimes Bisipara people seemed quite casual about devatas, and they chattered about devatas being kept or discarded or replaced, almost—perhaps not so openly—in the way that people here talk about the cars they have owned. Tuta had an earlier devata, but it did not function well, so he got rid of it. Then, when a relative who lived in Dangolu died, Tuta went over there and brought back the present devata. Sometimes the disapproving part came to the fore and the tale became cautionary. Oruno's great-grandfather kept a version of Durga and got rich; but ten of his eleven sons died. Perhaps— I think it unlikely—members of the panchayat, having spent a hard day cleaning out the village, by the evening had exhausted their indignation and slipped back into the more casual and complacent attitude of "everybody does it." But I had not heard any expressions of indignation during the day; people did not seem to have punishment at the front of their minds. The atmosphere was very much "job to be done," not "someone will pay for this."

Another set of ideas about why the fines were small, coming from a different direction, is more persuasive. First, the panchayat was accustomed to bargaining with offenders. They wanted offenders to admit they were in the wrong, because they were hard put to carry out a sentence if an offender refused to cooperate. Obviously, the milder the sentence, the more likely it was to get the offender's agreement. Furthermore, given the overriding concern with community harmony, it made good sense to have offenders acknowledge their guilt and let them resume their normal places in society. Second, on this particular occasion, the offenders were in a strong bargaining position. What they had to offer—an admission of error—found itself a sellers' market. All the leading men of the village, indeed everyone, including the offenders themselves, had a strong interest in getting the matter settled that same night. If that was done, they could make a clean start to Sri Ramchandro's birthday celebrations.

Despite the protestations of Tuta's wife, the case did seem to be settled. The fines were handed over and banked with the fund that supported Sri Ramchandro's temple. There remained only two tasks. One was to clear the offending devatas out of the village. The other, when all the work was done, was to deactivate the charpoy; to remove Bhuani's presence from it.

Back in the street, in front of the sirdar's house, four young men picked up the charpoy again. Two of those who had begun the day were back. The other two original carriers had gone home, exhausted and with blistered palms. One of the handlers on this final round was the adolescent son of Tuta, perhaps another indication that what Tuta had so far done was less heinous than I had thought. Or perhaps the sins of the fathers did not attach themselves to the sons. That was unlikely. Sons quarreled with fathers sometimes—usually very bitter quarrels, since in Bisipara youth owed deference to age—even formally disowning one another. But there had been no squabble known to me between Tuta and his son. Furthermore Bisipara people were used to the idea that an individual not only represents his group—household, lineage, village—but even, in certain contexts, *is* nothing apart from his group. A year later one of Tuta's sons, who had a clientele in the village across the river (I do not know if he was the handler on the night of March 21), lost that business because of the bad reputation that fell on the family as the Bisipara affair intensified and became more widely known. But that evening no one objected to the boy's handling the cot. The most likely explanation is that, first, he was standing around available, and, second, with the fines paid, the villagers considered the whole legal side of the matter closed. Blame had been apportioned and acknowledged; harmony had been restored.

The dehuri accompanied Bhuani to the five houses where malignant devatas had revealed their presence. At each of them he held out a brass dish that contained a confection of lia and molasses, molded to the shape of a narrow pyramid. The invocation enticed each devata from its place in the house or garden and located it in the charpoy along with Bhuani. His intention was to unload them all in the forest.

When the charpoy had its charge of devatas, the party returned to the sirdar's house. The dehuri received five rupees and a *gamucha* ("napkin" in my dictionary, but actually a towel or shawl-like cotton cloth). These are quite cheap; at that time they cost about a rupee. The weave is thick and strong, and we used them in the household as tea cloths and face towels. They are a practical addition to everyday life. On cold mornings they can be wrapped around the shoulders (which is why I call them a shawl). They are bound around the head, like a turban, or hung loosely, like the head part of a burnoose, when people have to walk in the sun. They can be used to wipe away sweat. Small quantities of grain or other stuff can be tied up in them and carried, in the hand or on the end of a stick. I also saw them used to strain tea, which in Bisipara is brewed by boiling up tea leaves, powdered milk, and sugar all together in a pot and then straining the mixture into glasses or brass drinking vessels.

No doubt the gamucha given on that occasion to the dehuri ended up being used in some of those ways, but the giving of it has a meaning. The gamucha is the least of the clothes—the outer clothes—that people wear. Women wear the silver waist-belt that I saw on the dying Susila. Into the belt is tucked the end of a sari, a cloth about twenty inches wide and four or six yards long (sometimes longer), which is wound around the body to form a knee-length skirt and continued as a shawl to cover the upper part of the body. Women rarely wore a blouse. Men wore a dhoti, a three-yard length of cloth, tucked around the waist and passed between the legs from front to back and tucked up in the waistband. They wore no undergarment. They also had a shorter cloth, a *lungi*, which is wrapped around the waist and hangs, like a long skirt, to the ankles. This, in Bisipara, had the status of a bathrobe and was not worn in public, as it is in south India. On their upper bodies men had long shirts with side pockets, or sometimes a shorter version, these being the only stitched and cut garmets normally worn by either sex. If working, men wore nothing above the waist, except perhaps a gamucha around their shoulders or over their heads. Very small children went naked. About the age of three or four little girls acquired the belt and cloth to cover their genitals. People taking a bath, which they did every day, washed out their clothes at the same time. The larger garments, saris and dhotis, also went periodically to the Washerman. No everyday cotton garment lasted longer than a year.

A gift of clothing is a marker of status. The phrase in use for installing a man in the office of sirdar was to "bind the sari" on him. (In this instance the sari is a turban, not the woman's garment.) In the various celebrations that occurred through the year, for example when the first harvest was brought in or on certain days dedicated to a deity, the master of the house gave clothing to his servants, and all the family received new clothes. A customary form of contract with a man hired to work the season on a farm stipulated, besides food and sometimes a cash payment, how often the servant would receive new clothes. Those attending a wedding or a betrothal or a funeral contributed, besides food and sometimes cash, a dhoti or a sari for the person who was the centerpiece of the ceremony, the bride or the groom, the relict or the heir of a person who died. On these occasions new clothes signaled a new person. In general, the gift of cloth showed respect. That was the point of the gamucha given to the dehuri.

As well as the gamucha and the five rupees, which the dehuri presumably shared with his helpers from Dangolu, the village provided materials for a feast, rice and lentils, together with a chicken and a goat. A party of about twenty men assembled— some Panos, a larger group of Potters, and one Warrior, who was the dehuri for Bisipara's tutelary devata, and a few other men. They escorted the visiting dehuri and his party and the cot, which now bore both Bhuani and the troublesome devatas, out of the village. They walked south along a track that led them into the edge of the forest.

When that party was clear of the village, one of the Bisipara Potters, a gunia, went to "the four directions," Jaya said, and drove iron nails and spikes of wood into the pathways. The wood came from a tree that I failed to identify (it repels devatas, as garlic repels our vampires). From north, south, east, and west, the village was protected against the return of the malignant devatas. I asked Jaya to name the pathways. The nail to the south went into the path between the bungalow and Warrior street; the one to the north was up near the school; the remaining two were to the east and northeast of the village. The west was left uncovered; also many houses would be outside a line that joined the four nails. I pointed this out. Jaya was unconcerned. It was a matter of direction, not boundaries, he said; which by no means solved my problem. Once again their thinking escaped me.

To the north of Bisipara are its *bernas,* great areas (but mostly small fields) of terraced land irrigated to grow paddy. For the lower-lying fields the waters of a stream are captured, and water stays in them when the rains have ended. Their harvest is late— December and January—but, with luck, the yield is abundant. On higher contours, where the stream water cannot be led, fields are leveled and banked to hold water but are fed only by the rains. The harvest in them comes earlier, and the yield is less than in the stream-irrigated fields. Most fields are small; not many are larger than a tennis court. Small fields allow the drop from one to the next to be modest, and not so much earth has to be shifted to level the field. Fields become smaller still when divided between heirs; some are so small that it is hard to work a plow and a yoke of oxen in them. A narrow bank of earth separates one field from the next and holds in the water. Those banks are points of contention, because, it is said, owners try to shave a few furrows when plowing and so make their holdings larger. Nor is it unknown for the lower holder to sneak out in the night and let water drain from the higher field into his own. *Caveat agricola.*

No agricultural landscape more obviously bears the mark of domestication, of subservience to man, than a stretch of paddy fields. I cannot recall a single tree within any of the seven or eight bernas that stretched, most of them to the north, for more than a mile beyond Bisipara's houses. Big trees that provided fruit or shade—mango, for example, or jackfruit—are allowed to survive in the rough ground that separated one berna from another. That apart, there is no variety, no break in the pattern, so standardized and so repeated that, tuning out the irregular shape of the fields, I was reminded—an unlikely simile—of the unending sameness of municipal housing estates in Liverpool, where I grew up. The fields, whether bright with that almost luminous green of new paddy or dry and brown and cracked in the hot season, deliver the visual message of the government lines in Phulbani; here is the realm of control and order and certainty.

Separating the bernas, or (a few) rising like small islands in the middle of them, are stretches of land too rocky or too steep to be worked into terraces. Here trees and shrubs grow. On the edge of the berna, beyond the rain-irrigated fields, where the land rises toward the forest, are other fields that are not leveled and do not hold the rain. These are called *anto;* a leveled and irrigated field is *khetu.* In their anto farmers sow a variety of paddy that has a low yield but matures as early as the end of September, handy for those living at the margin. They also grow lentils there, and mustard, and sesame, and chili peppers, and sometimes millet. Forest animals and birds take their toll.

Beyond those fields lies the forest. Around Bisipara, where for hundreds of years the Konds have practiced slash-and-burn cultivation, the forest is mostly secondary growth. Konds still make these axe-gardens, which they call *dahinga.* In them they grow turmeric, the roots of which (resembling ginger in shape) are a

Harvesting, threshing, and winnowing pulses (mugo dal) grown in an unirrigated field (anto). The man wielding the fan is the sirdar.

lucrative cash crop. The bush is cut and burned; the few very big trees survive the burn. Turmeric root buds are dibbled into the ash-enriched soil. Sometimes dahinga are planted with lentils and mustard and cucurbits. By the second or third year, fertility is gone and the field, abandoned, reverts to jungle. They reckon fifteen to twenty years before another garden can be made in the same place.

The tree that dominates the forest is *sal,* the hardwood that they use to make charpoy frames, plows and harrows and other farming implements, yokes for oxen, ox carts, axe handles, the frames and beams of houses, and doors and door frames. The walls in some of the older and grander houses in Bisipara were constructed of solid planks of sal, up to two feet wide, laid edge to edge horizontally. Now it is hard to find such large trees, and the forest is reserved. A permit is needed before cutting a tree over a prescribed girth.

The men seemed to me to have a neglectful, even wasteful, attitude toward the forest. Walking to another village with three or four companions, or occasionally out with a gun in search of jungle fowl or peacock or deer, we would sit and rest in a forest glade. Not being comfortable, as they were, sitting on my heels, I would search out a place clear of ants and sit on the ground. My companions would squat on their heels, and, while resting, reach out with the light long-handled axes they always carried in the forest and, with casual expertise, cut down a sapling. If we stayed long enough, each man, seemingly without thinking, would have cleared a semicircle in front of him of anything that grew, up to two or three inches thick. Having grown up in an industrial town, where trees were precious, I asked why they did it. "Just cleaning up," Jaya said, as if they had been weeding a garden. There was no romance in their vision of the forest, as there was in mine. The untidy disordered jungle ranked as an eyesore when set against land that had been made orderly, subservient to man, like a garden or, above all, like a leveled and banked paddy field with its growing crop of precisely hand-planted seedlings. Untamed nature made them feel, I suppose, inadequate. In September, when the dawn-to-dusk labor of planting seedlings had been completed and the harvests were yet to come, Bisipara had a flurry of meetings to discuss "cleaning" the streets. They appointed supervisors, two for each street, and apportioned out the pathways between the streets. Yet, so far as I could see, the streets were not dirty. (They had no litter that did not quickly decompose, except potsherds.) But in September nature is abundant, and their concern was about the grass and weeds that grew in profusion along the edges of streets and up against fences and the edges of verandas.

In the hot season they set fire to the dry leaves that carpet the

Carrying home the harvest of paddy, using a bamboo pole and bamboo slings. From this field to the owner's house was about half a mile. I could not even raise this load from the ground. The laborer, hired for the day, is the middle of the three Herdsman brothers. The owner of the field stands to the left. He is Susila's father.

forest floor, and at night one can see wavelike lines of flame rolling slowly up the mountain sides. That, too, was a way to "clean" the forest. Besides, the pragmatic Jodu once told me, the rains wash the ash down onto the fields and help the crops to grow.

The forest provides many beneficial things. In times of shortage, they say, a person can survive for two or three months on its wild products. Romesh, having no special botanical knowledge, wrote out the names of one hundred and fifty plants that provided foods, medicines, and other useful things. The poor man's spinach (*sag*) grows wild in the forest. Bark can be stripped from a green sapling and twisted into a serviceable binding cord that has many uses. All cooking is done over wood fires (sometimes charcoal). Wood is cut in the forest and carried into the village in bamboo slings, like the one used by the Gonjagura Potter. Bamboo has a hundred uses: baskets, winnowing fans, sieves, lightweight doors or movable partitions, fish traps, rain hats, and handles for small tools. The men are expert with axes, of which they have half a dozen different weights, selected according to the task. Women help bring the wood in, or gather fallen branches, carrying heavy loads not in slings, as the men do, but on their heads. They walk with that same rolling gait that seems to make loads lighter. The forest also is the source for leaves. Most households own brass bowls and platters and pots, but much of the time—and of necessity when many guests are fed—food is served on leaf plates and in leaf bowls. Both are made by pinning leaves together with short slivers of bamboo or spines from a thorn bush. The bowls hold liquids without leaking (I never could see how the trick was done). After use they are discarded and, when the dogs or chickens have cleaned them off, lie around to be eaten by goats or end up on the midden, eventually to be compost for the paddy fields or the vegetable garden behind the house.

When crops are standing in the fields, which are unfenced, the village herdsman collects the cattle from each house and takes them up into the forest to graze where they can do no damage. (In 1953 a Herdsman widow was hired to pasture the goats separately.) Sometimes water buffalo are turned loose in the forest during the hot weather, when there is no work they can do on the farm. Rounding them up in early June is a delicate and sometimes dangerous operation, because by then they are half-wild. Farmers do not turn cows or oxen loose in that way, because they would be taken by leopards or the rare tiger. Three or four full-grown water buffalo are big enough, and nasty enough, to protect themselves. The forest does have its perils. I have the young Bisipara Herdsman's genealogy; an uncle and, some time before, his father were killed in the forest by a leopard or a tiger. A Pano who herded cattle for Panosai died the same way. Bears are less dangerous, because they prefer to get out of the way, but there are more of them. There are also snakes, most of them not dangerous, if one steps carefully; a few, like the king cobra or Russel's viper, are aggressive.

The forest also has its devata, Parvati in Oriya (one of the many names that the wife of Shiva carries) or Soru penu (the mountain deity) in Kui. Her priest in Bisipara is a Kond Potter, and once a year, in April, he sacrifices liquor and chickens to her in a grove to the southwest of the village. The purpose is to make the forest products plentiful and accessible and to guard people and cattle against its dangers. A warning sign that Soru penu is discontented and must be placated with offerings is the noise of a leopard growling in the night.

From the kitchen, to the house, to the compound, to the street, to the village, there extends a series of circumferences that decrease in their capacity to provide order and certainty. Beyond the village lie the irrigated fields, and then the upland fields, and then the forest itself. Between the village and the fields a break marks civilization's first boundary. Conduct noticeably reprehensible in the village is ignored in the fields. Out there people are not so markedly on stage and they relax some restrictions that respectability requires in the village. Concerns with caste purity are less to the front. Standards of modesty are lowered; women occasionally will fold down the top part of their sari to give themselves greater freedom of movement when weeding a field.

There is a still bigger break at the forest's edge; forest and village stand at the two ends, representing the extremes. At one end is order and civilization, things under control, certainty: but the forest is the place of uncontrolled and uncontrollable forces, the negation of the idea of an ordered community. Consequently, what is a threat to the community is suitably expelled to the forest. There they took the charpoy. The dehuri performed a rite with liquor to persuade the devatas to depart. The goat was slaughtered, and the blood spilled on the ground was an offering to them and any other deities around. The chicken was not killed but was released into the forest, where, Jaya said, it would be consumed by Bhuani. That finished, they took the carcass of the goat to a place across the river under the mango tree (where the following night the Bisipara people had their carnival meat) and they butchered it and cooked the rice and lentils and had a feast. Afterward the dehuri and his three companions walked on southward, home to Dangolu. The Bisipara people came back across the river, two men carrying the charpoy, which would be restored to its owner in Potter street.

The events of the day generated a somewhat excited interest among the villagers. The day Susila died people were very obviously moved by grief, anger, and concern. I seem to remember (there is nothing in my notes) manifestations of fear of the kind that was around in summertime in England in the days before the polio vaccine. But I saw no signs of those deep emotions on the day of the divination. I overheard Romesh and Chanti having an animated discussion about where Bhuani had gone and was likely to go. Usually, as befits interaction between a man and a woman of different castes, the woman an untouchable and the man of clean caste, each of them adult and married, they communicated when they had to around the bungalow in a quite minimalist style, as if the other were an object rather than a person. The poorer of the two Christian widows, a hanger-on of the more affluent Christian widow who lived at the end of Warrior street, was ordinarily reserved and self-effacing. But on that day she turned up at the bungalow and gave my wife an excited account of what she had seen. (Around me she wrapped her face in her sari and spoke only when I spoke directly to her. She and the old lady of the main Christian house were the only village women who regularly wore a blouse and the long ankle-length sari.)

Other people too seemed to be energized by what was going on. Part of their excitement, I suppose, was that sense of pleasurable apprehension that is felt when the world has gone (but manageably) out of kilter. The forest, so to speak, had in a small way invaded the domain of their orderliness. By the end of the divination the apprehension and the anger, so evident on the day Susila fell ill, had given place to a mood of confidence, one that proclaimed the world again under control; the faults had been detected and soon would be put right. People seemed, understandably, to find satisfaction in contemplating danger now overcome and in the past.

They were also an audience excitedly watching a chase—not so much wondering who would be caught, but, already knowing the appointed victim, waiting in smug, even gleeful, anticipation for Bhuani to pounce. They were watching a drama unfold; when they talked about what was going on, they used a tone that suggested they were regaling each other with an adventure story, a thriller, enjoying the suspense, anticipating the kill. Yet at the same time they did not seem in the least vengeful.

That slightly furtive pleasure soon dissolved into something more positive. On March 23 they began the celebration of Sri Ramchandro's birthday, to be followed, over the next two weeks, by the reading of the *Ramayana* and dramatic performances enacting episodes from Rama's life; his birth; his marriage to Sita; the marriage feast; his exile and sojourn in the forest; the abduction of Sita by Ravana; the fight between the brothers Balin and Sugri; and—the grandest of finales—Hanuman, the monkey king and son of the wind, Rama's ally, setting fire to the palace of Ravana, the demon king of Lanka. "They beat up Hanuman but they could not kill him. Then he told them that if they wrapped cloth around his tail and set it alight, he would die. But Agni—fire—is his servant, and when his tail was lit he skipped around Lanka and set it all on fire."

They call it the "Burning of Lanka Festival," and it brings a great throng of people to Bisipara. They erect Ravana's palace in the harvested paddy fields near the school. The palace is a wooden framework shoulder high, a hollow square twenty yards to a side, and within it they build another and taller square. Straw is tied along the top of the framework to represent a thatched roof. When they set it ablaze, it is indeed a spectacle.

On that last day of the 1953 festival the vendors of sweetmeats, who earlier had dug shallow trenches along the edges of Warrior street and lit fires in them to fry their food, shifted out to the

The throng of visitors at the Burning of Lanka Festival.

festival ground. Cheapjacks spread out mats and on them displayed things that seemed to me out of tune with the occasion: locks, combs, mirrors, razor blades, even sunglasses (earlier in the week I had seen several young men, most of them Panos, stumbling around in the dark wearing these unfamiliar things). There were sellers of green coconuts (sold for the milk in them), snacks of puffed rice (mudi) or puffed paddy (lia), cigarettes, and the village style of cigarette (bidi). There were "hotels" (tea stalls), men dispensing brightly colored fruit drinks in old bottles stoppered with a folded leaf, and makers of pan or betel (a plug of areca-nut parings, lime, and various spices, wrapped in a betel leaf; habitual chewers have mouths stained red and eventually lose their teeth). There were stalls that sold cloth and ready-made clothes: shirts and shorts for men and blouses for women. Many of the vendors were professional traders who made the round of weekly markets. In this way Ravana's make-believe palace had a

Ravana's palace burns. Sudersun, masked, appears on the left.

marketplace under its straw walls, repeating a pattern found in the erstwhile kingdoms that lay on the plains around the Kondmals.

There were several small bands of drunken dancers, men dressed as women, raggedly performing a courtship dance that Kond girls use to charm young men. I saw a drunken flirtation, two girls seated with their backs to a tree and brandishing long sticks, while two young men, each one holding a plate of lia behind his back, wooed them with a song. Each time the boys advanced within range, the girls whacked them with the sticks. I think they were Konds, who are less inhibited than Oriyas about the public display of amorousness. There was a secular wildness about the scene, a suggestion of conduct at the margin of decency, not at all characteristic of public behavior in Bisipara. A year later in a Kond village I saw the same licentiousness at a buffalo sacrifice (the ritual offering to Tana penu, the earth divinity: in former days a human sacrifice); nine-tenths of those attending, men and women, were staggering drunk. Conduct at the

Women selling mudi at the Burning of Lanka Festival.

margin in Bisipara bordered not on lasciviousness but on ecstasy. Drummers at a wedding sometimes brought that on. At Jaya's wedding I saw normally staid middle-aged Warriors, stone-cold sober but dancing wildly in a throng of Konds who had come to pay homage to the sirdar and his son.

On the morning of March 23, when the two-week festival was to begin, the preparations for Ramnobomi still were not finished. I sat on a veranda in Warrior street and watched four men making some repairs to the door of Sri Ramchandro's makeshift temple. Four or five adolescent girls, Susila's age, were working with a very old woman mixing mud with cow dung and plastering the low walls and floor of the area in front of the temple. Other men, all of them from clean castes and most from Warrior street, sat around on verandas or under the shade of a tall tree that grew near the temple, doing nothing; the exception was the sirdar, who, also sitting in the shade, was uncharacteristically vocal, busy giving orders and advice, urging everyone on to greater efforts and reminding them that time was short.

I returned in the early afternoon to my accustomed place on the sirdar's veranda. People had dressed for the occasion. Little girls who normally wore nothing but a strip of cloth now had saris wrapped around them. Boys who had run around naked in the morning now wore shorts or gamuchas that served as lungis. All clothes looked clean and new. Men wore shirts. Women's ears, pierced through the rim, were bent with the weight of gold rings; heavy dangling ornaments hung from the lobes. They wore silver collars and anklets and an armor of bracelets reaching halfway up their forearms. A few had blouses. Some wore the tie-dye patterned saris, rich in color and distinctive of Orissa, which are made in the Sambalpur region (and by Daiteri Mehera, a Weaver in Bisipara, who died the following year). Those saris appear only at weddings or on such occasions as this. Chanti wore one that cost thirty rupees, she told me proudly (in 1953 a good-quality workaday mill-made sari could be had for four or five rupees).

Sri Ramchandro's temple in Warrior street was in disrepair. As far back as 1947 the sirdar and another man had promised that together, as an act of piety, they would build a new home for Sri Ramchandro. They invited everyone to help and so share in the spiritual merit. The existing building was thereafter neglected, but nothing much was done to build the new one, beyond burning lime (cheaper than buying cement) and collecting stones and some wood. The monsoon rains and termites eventually caused the roof of the old temple to collapse, and in 1952 they demolished it. In January 1953 they laid the foundation stone for the new temple, but nothing more had been done by March, and once again they made use of a temporary structure erected on the site to serve during the Ramnobomi rituals. (I saw the new temple consecrated in 1955.) Some time before 1952, palm-leaf manuscripts and various other paraphernalia had been removed to another temple, which had been built many years earlier in Hatopodera by Chano Mehera, once a rich trader and moneylender but now old and poor. Each year, for Ramnobomi, these

Rites to lay the foundations of Sri Ramchandro's rebuilt temple. The central figure is the Gonjagura Brahmin. The figure seated to the right of the picture is Oruno the Brahmin. Bala, his inexpert younger brother, sits to the left.

objects were ceremonially restored to the makeshift building in Warrior street.

A procession of musicians and other men and the young Brahmin Ganesa, who cared for the Hatopodera temple and who was lucid on that day, went off to Hatopodera and returned, installing the palm-leaf books in the old temple. Inside, a Brahmin, hired from Gonjagura, officiated, aided by Bisipara's Oruno.

Men, some of them accompanied by small sons, came one by one, bringing offerings. I saw coconuts, a cabbage, papayas, and other fruits; and everyone handed over money. Those Panos who came—many did—set their offerings down on the ground beyond the canopy, joined their hands in a respectful greeting to Sri Ramchandro, touched their forehead with a hand and then put it to the ground, or got down and placed their forehead

Mrudungo players. All those present are Warriors. The player on the right is Sudersun, the sirdar's half-brother. The singer facing him, center right, is Jodu's second son, the one who suffered from constipation. The man standing far left at the back is Mithu, Kola Bisoi's heir.

on the ground. Men of clean caste walked into the canopied area and gave their offering at the door of the temple. Later a party of women came from Potter street, bearing plates of lia. Another party came from Warrior street (including women from the houses at its fringes: Herdsmen, Brahmins, Barbers, and the Washerman's wife) carrying a brass plate a yard in diameter heaped two feet high with lia. They too walked into the temple precinct, as far as its doors.

Pano musicians—drums, oboe, and tambourine—stood to one side. They alternated with another performer, a Warrior man playing the drum that is called *mrudungo*, the only one on which men of clean caste perform. It is slung around the neck and played with both hands, a high note to the right, the other end lower. It is a virtuoso instrument. Young men could be heard practicing on it late into the night. The mrudungo, along with small brass cymbals that are clapped together, accompanies devotional singing. In the hands of an expert, the drum seems itself able to talk and sing. It also sometimes produces manifestations of ecstasy in the performer or in the listeners.

The untouchable musicians, as I had seen happen at the divination and at Jaya's wedding, one by one had been replaced by more expert performers from Pano street. Again, they yielded without protest.

To someone grown accustomed to the style of Bisipara, this seemed a tranquil occasion. I was watching an act of worship, with all the calm and ordered regularity that we associate with Anglican or Roman Catholic church services. I thought I could even detect, in some of those sitting around, that faint air of boredom that goes with routinized ritual activity. Many of them, it seemed to me, were watching out for who came, and what they brought, and the fine saris and ornaments the women wore.

But other things were going on. I caught the end of a rapid argument between Oruno and Sripati Pradhan, the sirdar's henchman. Oruno was again making his plea to be restored to his privilege. "This is my privilege. Let me do it! This privilege should go to feed my stomach." It was too late, Sripati said, in the manner of someone clinching an argument, they had already hired the Brahmin from Gonjagura. (Ramnobomi was reckoned beyond the capacities of the syphilitic young man Ganesa and of Oruno's younger brother, Bala.) Oruno, Sripati said, should have spoken up sooner (which, in my hearing, he invariably had done, at every opportunity). Then a Brahmin visitor from another village intervened and, reminding them of the need for tranquility and harmony, arranged a compromise: Oruno and the man from Gonjagura would officiate together (as they were already in fact doing).

On the veranda of the house next to the temple, Jodu's son Suren lay on his stomach, pen in hand, ink bottle nearby, and on the ground in front of him a hand-stitched sheaf of papers (they make their own notebooks that way). In the absence of desks and tables, that was the posture that people adopted when writing. Next to him sat Debohari, overlooking what he wrote. Debohari was of the sirdar's faction, Suren of his father's party. As people arrived to make offerings, including some who had brought nothing to the temple, they came first to Suren and each handed over three annas. (There were sixteen annas to the rupee; India had not yet gone metric.) Debohari put the money in a brass dish. Suren wrote down the name and the figure three; Debohari checked that he did so.

One anna was the customary contribution from every household, along with several other sources of money, used to defray the costs of Ramnobomi. Two annas were to pay for the divination that had taken place two days previously.

Early in the proceedings, just before the altercation between Oruno and Sripati, I had seen another apparently small ruffling of the waters. The sirdar had summoned the five people fined on Saturday night—Oruno, Bagoboto Pradhan (Sripati's older brother), Syamo Dehuri from Potter street, Srimati (the spinster from Hatopodera), and Tuta—and, there in the open street where everyone around could bear witness, had returned their money to them.

6

The Conspiracy

Early on the morning of Monday, March 23, Sripati Pradhan came to the sirdar's compound with a tale to tell. The previous evening, he said, he overheard his elder brother, Bagoboto, talking with Syamo Dehuri and Tuta the Washerman. The latter two men must have walked out to New street, where Sripati and his brother lived. (They shared a common great-grandfather with Basu Pradhan, the Bisipara businessman who came with us to the hospital in Phulbani.) Bagoboto and the other two men were planning, Sripati reported, to go to court in Phulbani and make a case against the village over the fines imposed on them two days before. This they intended to do, in spite of having signed the document accepting whatever decision came out of the divination.

The sirdar sent Sripati across the street to tell Jodu, the leader of the rival faction, what was going on and invite him to discuss what should be done. (Jodu told all this to Romesh, who later told me.) The first thing, they decided, was to return the fines, which is what I saw being done that afternoon. The money would be handed back openly but without discussion or explanation. The next step, they agreed, would be to have the panchayat meet and double the fines; fourteen rupees for Tuta, and six each for the other two. Oruno and the spinster would get their money back as well, but the new meeting would reimpose only the original

three-rupee fine. If everyone paid up, that would end the matter. If they continued to deny keeping a devata, they would be
told to take an oath on the *Purana* ("the old things," the palm-leaf
manuscripts belonging to Sri Ramchandro's temple). The punishment would then—this is how Romesh put it—be left to Sri
Ramchandro. In any case, anyone who refused to pay the fine
would suffer the ultimate penalty; he or she would be boycotted.

The sirdar and his two companions, had they been asked,
would no doubt have said that this was not a kangaroo court.
They knew they were not making binding decisions; they were
just working out an agenda to put before the panchayat. Of
course, with the leaders of both factions backing it, and the sirdar
customarily deciding what the consensus of a meeting was, the
panchayat would hardly reject the proposal.

To me it seemed strange that a man should fink so unhesi-
tatingly on his own brother, and I asked Romesh if Sripati and
Bagoboto Pradhan did not get on well. The correct relationship
between brothers is trust and solidarity. An elder brother should
be like a parent, guiding and training and protecting the younger
brother, who in return owes respect and devotion. (A theme in
the *Ramayana* is devotion and rivalry between brothers. At the
time I missed the irony my question might have had.) But an
Oriya proverb says, "A brother is an enemy." It is a paradox that
highlights an unwelcome truth, for in real life brothers often do
not get along well. There are many reasons. The one favored by
Debohari, a gently cynical man, with whom I often talked about
family life, was straightforwardly materialistic. Brothers share
their father's property when he dies. Always they are jealous,
thinking the other has had, or is aiming to get, a better deal in
the partition. Moreover, if they have to divide a field, they become adjacent cultivators and get into fights about water or about
plowing the extra furrow to enlarge their own holding at the
other's expense. Wives make the situation worse. If they come
into a joint family, in which a man and his sons work their land
together and perhaps keep a common hearth, the wife is always
keen to separate her husband from his brothers and persuades

him to demand his share of the estate. Also, they quarrel with other wives, wanting more for their own children. That is what men say about women. Women, I suppose, do not see anything wrong about wanting more for their own children.

Sripati and his elder brother were middle-aged, their father dead, and the estate long since partitioned. They lived in neighboring compounds (there was more room to spread out in New street than in the old part of the village). The partition had been without marked acrimony, and there was no known enmity between the brothers. They played prominent complementary parts in the dramatic performance that very same evening and on subsequent nights, Sripati as a singer and Bagoboto as a director and prompter. Perhaps there was some enmity; I did not know the brothers well. If so, it was certainly not on the surface.

My next thought was that Sripati was looking after himself, even at his brother's cost. Sripati was one of the sirdar's henchmen. Perhaps that word is too strong; let us say he was one of the sirdar's subordinate allies (a phrase much used by nineteenth-century British administrators trying to make sense of the complicated and always-shifting alliances, enmities, and rank ordering of Orissa's feudal lords). Sripati was a skinny man—no one in Bisipara was fat, but many were muscled—whose appearance and demeanor made me think of the envious Casca; he had a lean and hungry look. He was gifted with considerable forensic skill and would argue with people in the panchayat, never at a loss for words, until they gave up or sometimes lost their tempers and became incoherent with rage. I saw him once do that to Kopilo, himself a practiced debater. The sirdar was a taciturn man, with little to say for himself until he judged that the moment had come to step in with his version of the sense of the meeting, delivered in an "I take it there can be no objection" manner, thus putting an end to further debate. The earlier running was made for him by others, often the eloquent Sripati.

The sirdar's patronage was worth having, and his enmity to be feared. There was an element, kept mostly below the surface, of "might is right" in Bisipara. Suren used that very phrase, in English, in the midst of telling me (in Oriya) how the place really worked. There were several fields attached to the bungalow where we lived, which was government property. They were allocated to the watchman (Chanti's husband) as compensation for his responsibilities (cleaning and doing minor repairs). But I had seen a laborer from the sirdar's household plowing one of the fields, which did not make sense. Why? Suren explained: "Might is right." It was a particularly good field. On the other hand I never found in Bisipara much evidence of the egregious violence that is a feature of agrarian bossism in some other parts of India.

Patronage was the normal state of affairs both in the village and beyond it. Bhuani, for example, was talked to and deferred to as a patron, invited and cajoled into doing favors. Basu Pradhan, making sure they got what they wanted at the hospital, was being a patron. So, inadvertently, was I. The sirdar was a patron all the time, and no one's client. So was Jodu. And so were some other men. They all had clients, and some of the clients had their own clients, in a chain of patronage, that elsewhere, but not yet in Bisipara, extended up and down from the village bosses to the leading politicians in the state. It was, as should be clear by now, a society that worked less through bureaucratic impersonality than through personal contact, and in particular through face-to-face relationships negotiated within the given framework of superior and inferior.

They gave to hierarchy the same unthinking acceptance that we sometimes give to equality. Neither Konds nor Oriyas have brothers and sisters; they have *elder* and *younger* brothers and sisters. So, of course, does everyone else, but in Bisipara they mark the difference by using distinct terms of reference and in some contexts treating elder and younger siblings as if they belonged to another generation. There is a concept in Bisipara that can be glossed as "brotherhood," and it does connote equality, but it is an equality of blood or of heritage, not the absence of power. All the Bisois, old and young, rich and poor, are a brotherhood. So also, in certain contexts, are all the men of Bisipara. It seemed to me that people in Bisipara were wary of any relationship that was not unambiguously marked by difference of power. Perhaps they thought those kinds of links dangerous because they saw them as things that are uncertain and still to be determined, unstable, poised always to slide toward rivalry and hostility. Perhaps the same line of thinking is present in the notion that only those untainted by the suggestion of equality can strike up a true friendship. Brotherhood is ambivalent. A brother really may be an enemy. A real friend is the *maitro*, the ritual friend who must belong to a different caste and therefore cannot be a kinsman and cannot be an equal.

The sirdar held a government appointment and was the government's agent not only in Bisipara but also in a wider domain, which was called a *mutha*. The boundaries of these muthas, of which there are fifty in the Kondmals, can be traced back to the territories of Kond clans. Sometime in the past, perhaps before the British came and certainly afterward, sirdars emerged as chieftains. They were both representatives of the government (in India called the raj) and at the same time themselves petty kings (rajas), in the model of the rajas of the little kingdoms on the plains, to one of whom the Bisipara sirdar's ancestors once owed allegiance. This feudal past was alive in the legends and histories that people still in 1953 told about themselves and their communities.

Whatever the true history, it was certainly the case that the sirdar's role had in it a touch of royalty. This feature did not reveal itself in everyday life; he dressed and he ate and he worked like any other well-to-do man in the village. Rather it was apparent in the attitude that people in Bisipara had toward him. He had authority. A sirdar is a kind of king, and in Hinduism the king stands for and is the guardian of dharma. In that respect he embodies the Divinity. The panchayat and the sirdar, mingled together in some mysterious way (he is the person who divines its will), are one of the foundations on which the community rests its orderliness and its existence. It therefore made sense for the Bisipara sirdar not to engage himself actively in polemical debate in village meetings.

That is the celestial part of the image; the other parts are more mundane. The sirdar is also the man who collects taxes for the government (and gets to keep two annas in the rupee). He is required to report serious wrongdoings to the authorities. He has the right to cultivate government lands allocated to him. He is, in short, not only a feudal lord but also a minor bureaucrat. (In the past some sirdars were themselves informal clients of senior administrators in the area, and in that way had much influence. By 1953 that power was gone, and in the new democratic India sirdars were officially stigmatized as "relics of feudalism and imperialism.")

Certainly the sirdars were relics of feudalism; the lineage name Bisoi is a title of service indicating control over a district, or a "fort-holder." But in 1953 the sirdars were still very active relics. For about a century they had been able to use their link with the government to enhance the rewards that feudal custom gave them. Such payments were called *mamuls*. The sirdar collected a few rupees when he adjudicated a case. He had a customary right to a gift when there was a wedding or a funeral in the household of one of his better-off Kond subjects. Konds contributed their presence and their gifts to major occasions in the sirdar's house, as I saw when hundreds of them came to celebrate the wedding of Jaya, the sirdar's eldest son. When the sirdar visited Kond villages, to hear cases or to collect taxes or even to do deals in turmeric, he expected to have food supplied for him and his entourage.

In most of what the Bisipara sirdar did in village affairs he was not a divinity above the fray, but an active, forceful, combative, and sometimes vindictive, politician. A particular source of conflict was the new temple for Sri Ramchandro. When the sirdar and the other man initiated the project in 1947, most people liked the idea and from time to time made contributions. As always in Bisipara, written accounts were kept, and the money was held at that time by a Distiller shopkeeper. When they had about seventy rupees in the fund—this story was told to me by Debohari, who shared a common great-grandfather with the sirdar

and belonged to the sirdar's faction—the Distiller left the village.
The sirdar said the money went with him, but there was some
doubt. Some years back Romesh and his father had kept accounts
for the Ramnobomi festival. When it was over there was a balance of sixty rupees. The sirdar borrowed fifty rupees to get his
bicycle repaired. Later, when the question of handing over the
balance to the temple fund came up, he claimed he had taken
only thirty rupees. The accounts were written at the time he took
the money, but he claimed they were mistaken.

On another occasion the sirdar (so it is alleged) pocketed sixty
rupees. The Christian house at the end of Warrior street was occupied by a respected elderly widow. She was respected because
she was rich, because she had a commanding personality, and
despite the fact that she was a Brahmin who, when widowed,
had married a Christian widower. Oruno the Brahmin was her
grandson. Her Christian sons were in fact stepsons. One of them,
a widower, was a man of about fifty, a somewhat eccentric and
reclusive person who, unlike his brothers, his son (the man who
had a university degree), and his nephews, had not made a career
for himself in commerce or in the administration. He stayed in
Bisipara and supervised cultivation of the lands that the family
owned there and in some Kond villages. One night, thinking he
heard a bear in the maize garden behind his house, he got out his
shotgun, loaded it with a ball cartridge, and shot the creature that
was lumbering around in the shadows outside. Unfortunately it
was not a bear, but the bull that someone had presented to the
Shiva temple and that, as bulls do in India, wandered at will
around the village. Because the man was a Christian, there was
no call for him to do penance; but he did compensate the village
by paying sixty rupees. That money too, Debohari said, his "elder
brother" the sirdar "ate." Why? Like most sirdars he was in continued trouble with the government because over the years, over
the generations, he and his predecessors had taken more than
the eighth that was their due from the taxes they collected.

Considerations of that kind, the sirdar's undoubted power and
his readiness to bend the rules, must have been in Sripati's mind

(so I imagined) when he chose to inform on his brother and the other conspirators. He was protecting his own position as the sirdar's client. But that was not the way Romesh chose to see the situation. Sripati was acting for the good of them all, he said, his brother included. It would be utter folly to involve the courts and the government in village affairs. The case would drag on for a long time, the costs would be formidable, and everyone in the village would be losers. Sripati had done the right and sensible thing, and if his brother and the Washerman and the rest of them would also be sensible, the matter could be kept in the village and it would all be done and finished in a few days.

The sirdar, along with Jodu and Sripati, had his plan ready to put before the panchayat, but no meeting was called until the next day. On Monday, March 23, the first of the Ramnobomi plays was scheduled to take place, beginning at dusk and going on until two hours after midnight. They might with some difficulty have held a meeting earlier in the day, but Monday, unlike the days that came later in the festival, was filled with activity from early afternoon onward. Instead, the panchayat met on Tuesday. I do not have a record of where they met or who attended. I suspect it was a rump-attendance, since yet another meeting was scheduled for Wednesday to "get everything settled."

At the rump meeting (if that is what it was) they filled out the sirdar's agenda. They had an access of tidy-mindedness—what prompted it I do not know—and decided to demand the same fine from all the offenders, except Tuta. They set it at four rupees. Perhaps some legalistic person argued they could not punish people for *talking* about going to court, only for actually doing so. Perhaps they did not entirely trust Sripati and suspected that he, fearing his brother might do something rash, had anticipated him by making up a tale of conspiracy, hoping the outcry would make Bagoboto think twice before going to court. Sripati's motivations, even his actions, remain distinctly murky.

Something else was going on that I still do not understand. They seemed, at this stage, reluctant to single out the offenders and treat them differently from one another, even Tuta. A few days later, with nothing yet resolved, people were saying it might be best to fine them five rupees each (thus arriving at the customary twenty-five rupee penalty) and so get the matter closed. At the Tuesday meeting, however, they were unwilling to lump Tuta in with the others, although that would have been logical for anyone who believed that Tuta could not have known that his devata would escape. If the offense was keeping a spirit that was *potentially* a public menace, they were all equally guilty. Tuta's fine, however, stayed at the larger figure, fourteen rupees.

The meeting also renewed and intensified threats about the punishment in store for any offender who did not accept the panchayat's decision. First the offenders must pay up, as ordered; fourteen rupees from Tuta and four from each of the others. There was no choice about paying up. At the same time they must put their names or their marks to a document admitting they had kept a devata and agreeing that they had been justly fined by the panchayat. But afterward, any offender who still claimed that he (or she) had not kept a devata, despite having just signed an admission to the contrary, could take an oath on the books in Sri Ramchandro's temple. Then everyone would wait and see what Sri Ramchandro did about it.

This seems a strange condition, because it disconnects Sri Ramchandro's justice not only from government justice but even from village justice. Nothing was said about returning the fine to anyone who took the oath and Sri Ramchandro declared innocent (or about how long they would wait for Sri Ramchandro to show his hand). Nor—which seemed to me would have been logical— was there ever any question of making the oath and the payment of a fine alternatives. It is logical because it would have meant that paying up was an admission of guilt; and an oath that denied guilt but was made in bad faith would eventually bring down on the person the fate of Gopi's father who came to Ramnobomi drunk. But the panchayat's move does make sense if one assumes that they firmly believed the parties were guilty and equally firmly believed they would not dare swear an oath. This challenge—to swear to their own innocence—was made several times during the affair, but none of the offenders in fact took the risk. The challenge scored a moral point for the panchayat; the offenders, whatever they said about themselves, tacitly admitted their guilt by refusing to leave the decision to Sri Ramchandro.

Another certificate was to be written out and signed by everyone in the village agreeing that if the offenders did not pay the fines and admit their guilt in writing, they would be boycotted. Neither this document, nor the one to be signed by the offenders, was drawn up at the time. Nor was any money paid over. That is why I suspect the meeting was not well attended. The offenders themselves may not have been present. Two of them, Bagoboto and Syamo Dehuri, played a major part in the nightly performances. Oruno the Brahmin, now insecurely restored to his position as the officiant in Sri Ramchandro's temple and busily supervising and sharing in the recitation of the *Ramayana*, could also have been engaged elsewhere. The Tuesday meeting closed with a resolution that the panchayat would assemble again the next day and see to the paying of fines and the signing of documents.

The mind-set that appears to put such faith in written documents borders on the realm of magic. Sometimes it is straightforwardly magical and easily comprehended by outsiders like ourselves, for there is no culture that does not reinforce its oaths with sanctity. As we take oaths on the Bible, they swore on the palm-leaf books that celebrate Sri Ramchandro's life. Other instances are not magical at all; they are plain common sense, as when they insisted on keeping a written record of contributions made to village funds. The panchayat did not hand out receipts (government agencies, including the sirdars, were required to do so), but the notion of a record of payment was familiar and considered a necessity. In matters of commerce and money Bisipara people were as rational as any neoclassical economist could wish. Only a fool would not cheat on a deal, they believed, given the chance to do so. (I have a long list of tricks that traders used to cheat Konds who grew turmeric, and others that the Kond growers used to trick the traders.) They also kept written records—when there was someone around who could write—of contributions that people brought to weddings or funerals or other occasions in the family, so that they could reciprocate appropriately when their turn came. Keeping a tally on the material value of gifts may not be entirely in accordance with our spirit of giving, but we surely see nothing irrational about doing so. (In fact we do it too, less blatantly and less exactly.)

But words on paper also had other kinds of significance in Bisipara. Surely part of this was the awe that writing inspires worldwide in those who are themselves not literate or who are unused to working with documents. We have proverbs about the mightiness of the pen, a strength that comes not only from the manipulative and organizational capacities that are open to those who know how to store information, but also from the simple veneration that is accorded to the written word—as in the case of the Bible or of Sri Ramchandro's *Purana*. But, in the Kondmals and no doubt in other parts of rural India and elsewhere, the belief that the written word is a means to dominate and exploit is given immediacy for ordinary people by their experience with the bureaucracy, and in particular with legal institutions. Documents are a symbol of power, if not power itself. To gain access the ordinary person needs Basu Pradhan or someone else whose face is known to officials and clerks, but the machine itself, once access is gained, can be made to work only by feeding it documents, the written word, petitions and writs and memoranda and, the controlling device, files. If your file does not "move," nothing happens. No document, or the wrong document, or the document with a mistake in it, sends a petitioner away empty-handed.

This notion, which is mostly tacit, would explain the panchayat's frequent recourse to having people sign their names to an agreement that, from a legal standpoint, binds no one. They are making an attempt to borrow the power that resides in paperwork in government departments. The gesture has its irony, for in some cases the device is used to discourage people from exercising the right they have as citizens to use the government courts.

That is the force of documents signed before a panchayat hears a case, making the litigants—or defendants—agree not to appeal to government courts and to pay a fine to the panchayat if they do so. Alternatively, a document accepting a verdict—as was proposed at the Tuesday meeting—is thought to stymie a successful appeal, for—it is wrongly assumed—the courts will recognize an appeal as a breach of contract and so dismiss the case.

But on this occasion no documents were drawn up and signed, neither by the offenders nor by all the villagers, and no fines were paid, because the meeting scheduled for Wednesday was not held. I did not notice this until two days later, for I spent most of Wednesday night in Warrior street watching the play, and watching the audience watch the play.

Mats had been spread on the ground opposite the temple doorway. They were occupied by men and boys from clean castes. Near them sat a man playing the mrudungo and around him four or five others accompanying him on small brass cymbals. The man playing the drum wore a nonstop expression of ecstasy. He was a virtuoso performer who journeyed from village to village, spending a week or two giving expert instruction to the young men. To the right of the men was a much larger group of women and small children, all of clean caste. The women sat still; but men would stand up from time to time, stretch themselves, wander away, and then come back. (The memory of that scene recalls Sunday morning in an Alpine village where I lived. The men hang around the plaza and doorway of the church, while their wives and children are inside attending Mass.) On the opposite side stood the Pano musicians, silent; they had been playing since around six o'clock, and it was now near to ten. Behind them squatted a crowd of men, women, and children from Pano street.

The occasion was the marriage of Rama and Sita. The players—all men or boys, including Sita the bride, who was played by Jodu's second son, the constipated one—used Mithu's house, which adjoined the temple, as their dressing room. The masked faces were elaborately made up, enormous curling moustaches for the men and exaggerated eye makeup for the "women."

Their clothes were rich indeed: silver-threaded tunics, green silk trousers, fine turbans, peacock feathers for the males and silk saris for the females. The players emerged into the light of pressure lanterns (mine and the sirdar's and one borrowed from the shopkeeper) and sang. They required frequent prompting from Bagoboto, who sat to one side reading a script (a palm-leaf book) by the light of a hurricane lamp. The principal singer, not playing a part but acting as a narrator, was the lean Sripati; the mrudungo player and the cymbal players accompanied him, from time to time singing back to him as a chorus. The audience, at this stage, seemed somewhat inattentive; there were a lot of quiet conversations, and the men were still coming and going.

They were more attentive when the marriage ceremony was performed. This was done around a ceremonial hearth and fire as in normal marriages, and the two Brahmins, Oruno and the man invited from Gonjagura, officiated. The bride arrived with an escort of Pano musicians, just as brides arrive in Bisipara, and, as sometimes is done in real life, a muzzle-loader was fired into the air. (Jaya did this, succeeding on his third attempt after two misfires, and a long time after the anticipated place in the ceremony. It made people jump.) Everyone was now awake and attentive, but they did not seem to lose themselves in the performance until the comedy began. Oruno and his companion were interrupted and impeded and given advice and mimicked by three men playing Brahmin priests, each with a false pigtail stuck on the back of his head. Another popular character was a man in a grotesque mask who kept coming out of the shadows to demand when the feast was going to begin. They kept sending him away, and he kept coming back to ask the same question. There was also someone in attendance to make fun of the barber, an unkempt, disheveled buffoon, brandishing a large pair of toy scissors and a wooden razor.

Bisipara's star comedian was a Distiller, Madhu Sahu, the man whose mother had died not long before. From time to time he rode in on a hobby horse, to the delight of the children. Later he appeared with two little boys, each on the end of a string (one of them was the son over whom his mother wept when, in 1959, she told me of his death). They were his monkeys; I had seen such performances with real monkeys in Cuttack, Orissa's only large city. Madhu stamped his foot to keep time and made the boys dance, bawling at them in very bad Hindi. I saw him on another occasion perform in a Saville Row suit, the relic of some departed Englishman. It was much too big for him, but with padding stuck in it to give him an enormous belly, a solar topee on his head, and brandishing a walking stick, leading a little dog (a Skye terrier), he was the perfect sahib, the Englishman—with a genuine "foreign" dog quite unlike the rangy and ferocious mongrels that were the norm in Bisipara—barking out stupid orders and singing a song, the chorus of which I remember: "Look at my belly! Just look at my belly!" The *Ramayana* re-enacts human dilemmas: fathers and sons, husbands and wives, brothers and their tribulations. Bisipara had imported satire and brought it almost up to date, lampooning British administrators. Perhaps by now, forty years later, their targets include vote-seeking politicians and the bureaucrats who handle rural development and men on the make like Basu Pradhan.

When the marriage rite, prolonged but enlivened by all these interruptions, was complete, the sirdar came forward and put a coin in a brass plate that lay on the ground before the altar. Then he joined his hands, palms together in front of him, in the gesture of respect, the *namaskar*. He was followed by his son's wife and a woman of his compound who stood to him as a younger sister (we would call them cousins), the only woman of that generation not yet gone in marriage. They too made namaskar and put a coin in the plate. Then followed a procession of women, each doing the same. Half an hour passed before the giving was completed. (The amount contributed was four rupees and seven annas. It was divided between the two Brahmins and the village Barbers—the real ones, uncle and nephew, not the comic.) It was now one o'clock in the morning. The drama continued for another hour. Ram and Sita built a house and lived in it (a length of cloth wrapped around three sticks stuck in the ground). Then Ram and Porsuram had a battle. Ram won and Porsuram fled.

Why did they fight? They fought, Kopilo said, because that is what heroes do; it is their dharma, their nature.

On Thursday they held the wedding feast. They brought us, as they did for ordinary weddings, a share of the food (uncooked)— rice, dal and vegetables, no meat. In the evening, when the sun had gone down, I went for a walk in the brief Indian twilight. Fires were being lit in Warrior street and men were getting ready to cook the meal. Each caste had its place and its own fire: the few Brahmins in front of Sri Ramchandro's temple; Potters to the west and Distillers to the east of the mandap; the Warriors near the sirdar's compound. There were no Panos from the old street. Chanti and the Pano musicians later collected food, already cooked, from each group. The rice and the lentils came from fields that Sri Ramchandro owned and rented out to sharecroppers.

There was no play that night. "People say," Kopilo explained, "that's because Dasarath the king, Sri Ramchandro's father, died that day, and so you wouldn't put on a play." He was skeptical. "That's what people say," he added, "but who knows if that is when he died; it doesn't say so in the *Ramayana*. He could have died any time." Kopilo took the whole affair in his old man's stride. I asked if he fasted on the first day. "Me?" he said, "Of course not. I'm an old man. I've got a son to do the work." Did he go to the wedding play? (Romesh had told me the panchayat could fine you for not attending.) No, Kopilo went to bed. Old men put themselves in a condition that in Bisipara they called *bonobasi*, "dweller in the jungle," the third stage of a Hindu life, withdrawing themselves from worldly activity in preparation for the final stage, the ascetic life of a *sannyasi*. No one in Bisipara actually lived out this fourth stage, which involves a literal withdrawal from the community, living as a mendicant. I did, however, know a senior civil servant (the man with a doctorate in anthropology), who, when he retired from the service, withdrew to sit on a mountainside in the Himalayas and died there. I know exactly what he did, and why he did it—at least, I can expound the values and traditions that lay behind his action. In a deeper empathetic sense I do not understand such behavior at all.

In a similar way, when Ramnobomi had come and gone and I

had time to reflect, I was still having trouble understanding the divination and its aftermath. At one stage I thought I had the matter intellectually domesticated by comparing it to an outbreak of a half-understood epidemic disease, something like the infantile paralysis that marked my childhood summers. Lives were at stake, one never knew where the disease would strike next, there was good reason to be frightened. But feelings of that nature and of that intensity were manifest only at the beginning, the day Susila fell ill and the day she died. The divination seemed to do its job; it provided reassurance. As the charpoy went on its rounds the apprehensions of the earlier days gave way to an almost pleasurable excitement, an interest in the procedure itself, and speculation as to whom it would uncover (more accurately, when it would uncover them). The dangers that the ritual was intended to avert seemed to be forgotten.

My psychological speculations were followed by reflections on what these events told me about the nature of the community. Individual fears, people apprehensive for themselves or their dear ones, were in the beginning real enough, but they coexisted with and gradually were dispelled by a process in which the community was putting itself back in order, restoring harmony. I was familiar, from my reading about other places, with the idea that quasijudicial processes, such as I saw in the panchayat, were less intended to pin down offenses and punish offenders than to get the community's values—fertility, prosperity, good health, and the like—onto the front stage, where everyone could see them and acknowledge them and celebrate them, and tell each other that all would be well again. Thus I was able to make sense of what seemed a ridiculously disproportionate penalty for causing the death of two children (if that is what they really believed). I could also understand why the offenders were allowed—indeed expected—to play their normal parts in everyday affairs: why Tuta's son could be one of the charpoy's handlers; why all the offenders were allowed to work in the Ramnobomi sequence (except Srimati the spinster, who would not have had a part anyway, being a woman). The several comments that I heard about getting the affair tidied away also fit well into this frame. Dissension was bad, people said, dangerous both for the community and for the well-being of the people in it, and doubly so in the two weeks of Ramnobomi. That was why the divination was so promptly arranged. Susila was cremated Thursday morning. By Saturday they had brought a dehuri, completed the divination, cleared the bad devatas out of the village, held a meeting to assess blame, and collected fines from the offenders. All, apparently, was clear for Monday's opening of Ramnobomi.

But all was not clear. The drive to restore harmony was not entirely successful, and certainly a desire for harmony will not explain why the witch-hunt got under way again as early as Monday morning. The explanation that would have seemed the right one to Jaya, and probably also to more skeptical persons such as Kopilo or Debohari, was that the offenders not only had failed to repent, acknowledge their guilt, and return to the fold, but also had put the community in peril in another way, by planning to embroil it with government agencies. I do not know whether the three men—Bagoboto, Syamo, and Tuta—really did intend to go to the government courts. That had been done in the past, and government intervention was invited in Bisipara the following year, when there was a mild outbreak of civil disorder between the clean castes and the Panos who lived in the old street. But in the case of these three men, it seems to me most unlikely that they would have gone to court: none of them was rich enough to be effective in that arena; none of them had the kind of contacts they would need even to make a start. These facts and their significance were surely known to other people in Bisipara, especially the leading men of the panchayat.

But it might still be the case that they actually did *threaten* to go to court, without ever intending to do so. This was, after all, a well-known tactic in bargaining with the panchayat. But that too seems unlikely. With fines set at seven rupees for Tuta and three rupees for the others (except Bagoboto, who had already bargained his down to two rupees), there would not have been much point in starting up a haggle again. Perhaps, as I said,

Sripati made it up; or perhaps he misheard. Or perhaps he, and some others with him, while announcing, like everyone else, that they should put the matter behind them as soon as possible, in reality wanted to keep it alive. That raised the question for me, if the suspicion was correct, of who wanted to keep it alive and why they wanted to do so. One wonders in particular whether they, whoever they were, saw some private gain coming out of continuing the witch-hunt, or whether they felt that the first divination had been botched and that lives in Bisipara were still being endangered by a rogue devata.

The answer to that last question seemed to be conclusively given by an incident that, for a short time, marred the performance on the night of Saturday April 4. The young wife of Sadhu Bisoi (one of the men who had transferred allegiance from Jodu's to the sirdar's faction), while sitting in the middle of the group of women watching the players, was suddenly seized by a devata. She screeched, louder than the music and the performers, staggered to her feet and ran into Tuta's house, which was about thirty yards away. The unfortunate Tuta had a fever and was lying on a mat on the floor. She took hold of his feet, which is an accepted way to ask for the indulgence of a powerful person, and screamed. Several people followed her into the room. When Tuta, by now terrified, realized what was happening he protested that there was no devata. They could look around the room and see. Nonetheless they insisted he fill his mouth with water and blow it over the woman, to cool the devata. This he did, and the woman collapsed, still conscious but unable to stand. Her husband and her mother, who was visiting for the festival, supported her and took her back to their house. Soon after, the two gunias from Potter street came and blew water on her, trying to make her well again. In the street the play continued.

Kopilo, reflecting on the incident, was reminded that a year earlier the young wife of another Warrior, Sudersun, the youngest half-brother of the sirdar and living in the same compound, had gone into a fit that lasted on and off for three days, screaming and crying and sometimes going rigid. In one of her lucid moments, so he had heard, they asked her what was wrong and she replied, "Bagoboto Pradhan is my father," which, translated, meant that his devata had seized her.

In her case there were other episodes of hysteria. Jaya, who lived in the same compound and himself had a new wife, said that such attacks were not unknown when a woman first came from her father's house to join her husband's family. A gunia could usually deal with the situation. "Could my medicine?" I asked him. "Of course it could," he said, sounding surprised. Later in the year when Sudersun's wife had another attack, Jaya came to ask for aspirin. I also have a memory, but no notes, of a conversation with him, in which he seemed to pattern possession by devatas in the way I patterned malaria. Those who come to a new place, as virtually all married women do, are more likely to be afflicted than those who have grown up there. After women have lived in their husband's village for a time, possessions are less frequent, and they rarely occur in the case of older women.

The affliction is not malaria, which is found everywhere in the Kond hills, and which, so far as I know, is not so localized that different strains are peculiar to different villages. The affliction rather is the miserable experience that many women have when they move in marriage to their husband's village. An expectation of misery in that situation is fully and explicitly built into the culture. When a girl leaves home she sings a lament: here, in her father's house, she is loved; there they will hate her and despise her, and be contemptuous of the dowry that she has brought. Her husband's mother will be cruel to her, and his sisters will bully her. Both Kond and Oriya brides sing in this fashion. Sometimes the new bride's life does turn out that way, sometimes not that way at all.

The notion of romantic love is not unknown to Bisipara people, but it is not salient in the married relationship. Very few people had seen a movie. The devotional literature of which they are aware emphasizes not love of that sort, but a wife's adoration for her husband. Certainly the idea that marital love transcends all obligations, and should be seen to do so, would have been considered bizarre. No public affection is ever shown between husband and wife. Quite the reverse; good manners require them to display emotional distance. Friends who visited us, recently married, scandalized Bisipara by walking hand in hand through Warrior street. They could hardly have caused more embarrassment if they had lain down in the dust and made love.

Even when people are kindly in their disposition toward the new bride, structural realities make for tension. The new bride is her mother-in-law's rival for the affections and attentions of the man, threatening to deprive the mother of the son whose birth gave her standing in her husband's house. Until a son is born the new wife is, as it were, on probation. A wife is also, convention has it, the source of dissension between brothers in a joint household; her manipulations break up the family. If, as most young married people do, they quarrel, she is without allies or support. Beating a wife (not too frequently and in moderation) is nothing shocking. When, as often is the case, this conventional wisdom approaches reality, it is small wonder that a few women find relief in being possessed by a devata.

Even without these structural tensions and the painful emotions that go with them, a married woman's life is hard. Each morning she rolls up the sleeping mats and hangs the cotton sheets over a beam in the courtyard. She kindles the fire and makes tea, if they can afford it. Then she sets out portions of lia or mudi (parched paddy or parched rice, made as we make popcorn). After the husband and children have eaten, she cleans the pots from last night's meal, feeds the baby, and sends the older children out to play in the street. She sweeps the courtyard, cleans the cowshed, and takes the muck out to the fields. Then she bathes and, returning home, climbs up to the big storage baskets and measures out paddy to be boiled and husked for the next day. She cooks the noontime meal, boiling a pot of rice over the fire in the courtyard, and preparing lentils and vegetables over another cooking place, usually inside the main room, which can get unpleasantly hot. A cooking fire burns in an ingenious roofed-in trench, with a high-lipped hole at one end on which to place the pot, and at the other a downsloped ramp into which the wood is fed. The arrangement produces a very effective draft for the fire. Women are red-eyed when they cook in the main room, because there is nowhere for the smoke to escape except through the doorway or the thatch. After the meal, everyone rests. Then, until the time comes to make the evening snack, which is usually cold leftovers from the noontime meal, a woman returns to work. Cooking is considered the lightest of her tasks, and it is the custom to favor a new bride by allowing her to be the cook.

Other work is physically more demanding. Women boil paddy (keeping the fire going for two hours) and later husk it, a task they find exhausting. They work in pairs at a heavy wooden contraption, a roughly shaped beam of sal wood about six feet long, hinged near one end on a wooden pin in a frame twelve inches from the ground. At the other end of the beam is a thick wooden pin, set at right angles like the head of a hammer. Under the hammerhead and let into the ground is a hollowed wooden socket, into which they put the grain. One woman stands at the short end of the beam near the fulcrum, hanging on to a rope slung from the roof, and works the beam with her foot, as we operate a foot pump. The work may last two or more hours, and they find it very tiring because the motion, applied from the short end of the beam, has to be imparted against the leverage; the better-off households hire a servant to do the work. The mistress of the house squats near the grain, sweeping it in and out of the hole with her hand. Very occasionally they misjudge the timing and sustain crushed or broken fingers. The work is done to a steady rhythm, and its regular thumping is one of the sounds, like the young men practicing on the mrudungo, that I can still hear in my mind. (A third one is the plough bird, *nangeli pota* in Kui, which in English is nicknamed the brain-fever bird. Its song is a rising succession of three-note frenetic shrieks that suggest a mind projecting itself into madness.)

Requiring less energy, but still tiring, is the task of grinding spices. A woman also prepares the cement of mud and cow dung to repair patches in the walls or the floors; she fetches water from the well and wood and leaves from the forest; she makes leaf plates and cups; and she works in the garden behind the house. From June until January she spends most of her day in the fields, transplanting paddy seedlings, weeding, and eventually harvesting. If she is fortunate she has a young daughter or an old mother-in-law who will cook; otherwise she must scamper back to the house to get meals ready.

Apart from that work in the fields, a woman spends most of her time in the house and the courtyard, which she leaves only to fetch water, to bathe in the river, to take muck to the fields, or to borrow a utensil or fire from a neighbor. A man can stroll around, stopping to chat with other men sitting on their verandas. A woman in the street should be a woman going on an errand.

Sadhu's wife was possessed on April 4. There were no meetings to discuss this new evidence of the continuing presence of a rogue devata. (They still had not held the final meeting originally arranged for March 25.) The festival continued, and the final great spectacle—the burning of Ravana's palace—took place on Monday, April 6.

On the night of April 4, after the play had finished, Tuta, despite his fever, fled from Bisipara to take refuge in the village where his brother lived. (As it happened, it was that same Dangolu from which the dehuri had been brought two weeks earlier.)

7

Tuta's New Penalty

The "brother" who lived in Dangolu was Tuta's father's elder brother's son. Tuta and the brother both had lived in Bisipara once, Kopilo told me, sharing the "privilege" of being Bisipara's Washermen. Ten or more years ago they got into a quarrel with the sirdar and they both ran away from the village, Tuta to one of his wife's relatives in a village called Rotungo and the brother to Dangolu. The brother stayed away, but after a time Tuta returned to Bisipara and took up his work again. I asked what the quarrel was about, but Kopilo did not know. If they had fled, taking their families, I reasoned that it could hardly have been a trivial matter. Could it have been about keeping a devata? No; it wasn't that. Tuta's paternal uncle had kept a devata, Kopilo said (reaching back a generation), but there was never any trouble about it.

Later I realized that the quarrel might not have been a matter of life and death, of imminent violence, as I had imagined. It could well have been only the occasion, not the main cause, for the brothers' leaving Bisipara to take a job elsewhere. There was in fact a market, albeit infrequently activated, for the services of Washermen and Barbers and Herdsmen and other specialists, including Brahmins. When Chano Mehera the Weaver, many years earlier in the days of his prosperity, built the temple in Hatopodera, he imported a Brahmin, Nityananda Panda, to serve it. When Nityananda died, the panchayat, now responsible for the temple, appointed his younger son Ganesa to do the work. Ganesa later went soft in the head but still functioned on occasions. The widow, Ganesa's mother, still lived in Hatopodera. Her elder son, Ramchandro, married and vigorously healthy, of sound mind but limited intelligence, was reckoned too stupid to handle the rituals. (He evidently had some compensating qualities. He seduced his brother's wife and, when the Bisipara panchayat intervened at Ganesa's request, took off with the two women, who were sisters, to live with their parents in Phiringia. He came back quietly later, only to flee again in 1955 when the villagers, hunting for those whose sins had brought on the drought, targeted him for twenty-five rupees.)

Bisipara's Herdsman, too, was a recent appointment. A young man as yet without a wife, he had taken the place of an uncle killed by a tiger. Accidents of that kind seldom befall other specialists. But they all die, and some of them die without a son to take their place. Then the panchayat looks around in other villages for a Barber or a Washerman with sons to spare. Also, specialists sometimes fall out with the panchayat that employs them. Oruno the Brahmin had that problem for a time. The Bisipara Panos (the original group that had come from Boad) had been dismissed en masse from their ritual privilege of music making and replaced by Gumsur Panos.

Thus the accidents of reproductive success and village labor relations can lead to a buyer's market or a seller's market. When one or another kind of specialist is in short supply, a panchayat is sometimes tempted to sweeten the offer and entice the man they want away from his job in another village. Conversely, when there are plenty of Barbers or Washermen or Brahmins available, the panchayat may tighten the discipline on their own village servant, making him toe what they think is the proper line, by threatening to bring in a replacement.

That kind of adversarial negotiation is not supposed to happen. Village servants, as I described earlier, are covenanted through a jajmani system. They are paid with a share of the harvest, and they receive food at the time of performing the service, and they

expect a gift of clothes on festive occasions. The service is notionally hereditary and the servant more closely resembles a family
retainer, part of a household, than someone hired to do a job.
Master and servant have a moral relationship, and market attitudes and the temptation to use scarcity to drive hard bargains
are neatly curtailed by the method of payment; since they share
the harvest, master and servant must share alike in good times
and in bad, and the share that each servant gets is fixed by custom. Furthermore, service is more than just doing that particular
job (cutting hair or washing clothes); it is a marker of status.
Rituals that go with marriage and death and other household
events require the work of village specialists. A household that
commands jajmani service is, by that very fact, a household of
standing. The service marks both full membership of, and high
status in, the community. On the other hand, refusal to provide
the service is a mark of exclusion, and when all the households
of a particular caste are refused, their claim to be a caste of high
status in the community is being rejected.

Most specialist castes, including the Washermen in the Bisipara
region, have a *samaj* ("meeting" or "association") that regulates
caste affairs. The samaj sets limits to bride-prices (a monetary gift
from the groom's to the bride's family), in a quite futile attempt
to counter inflation; any family that refuses to pay considerably
more than the "official" amount does not find a bride. (The official
Herdsman rate was then fifteen rupees. The following October
the three Herdsman brothers in Bisipara were haggling around
one hundred and twenty rupees with the father of a girl who
would be a bride for the middle brother.) The samaj also tries to
control the size of dowries (the wealth that a bride brings when
she comes to her husband's house), again without much success. It also prohibits customs that might lower the caste's status.
Herdsmen women, for example, were not allowed to deliver milk
to the police lines in Phulbani to save them from the importun-
ing that lewd men inflict on milkmaids. Occasionally elders of
the samaj are requested to settle disputes, which arise mostly in
the course of marriage negotiations. They fine people, haggling

as the village panchayats do. They have the power to outcaste, a serious punishment since the offender can no longer find a bride for his sons or a groom for his daughters. That does happen occasionally, but not often, since it requires, as in the case of the village panchayat, a widespread consensus. When it is done, the offender either goes far away to try to start life again or cajoles the samaj into allowing him to sponsor an expensive ritual to get himself restored to membership.

The samaj, people said, also watches over labor relations in villages. (That is the essence of what the elders attempt to do, but not the idiom they use.) If they consider one of their members unjustly penalized by a village panchayat, they forbid any other member from taking over his position. In theory, when they do that and if they are strong enough to make the decision stick, the village must either back down or look around for a Washerman (or Barber or Brahmin) who belongs to a different samaj. But in fact I never found a case of that being done.

One reason may be that households in a boycotted village have an interim remedy that can easily turn into a permanent solution. Services can be hired for the occasion. A caste samaj, which meets only infrequently and cannot easily be assembled at short notice, can do nothing about this kind of "strike breaking." Thus, with Oruno still under a cloud and his younger brother, Bala (his replacement), lacking the skills needed for the occasion, the village hired a Brahmin from Gonjaguda to run the Ramnobomi ritual. Any household that loses or cannot command specialist services under a jajmani arrangement can usually, provided it is of clean caste, pay ad hoc for whatever service is required. They get the work done, but they miss the increment of status. I owned no land and in any case, being outside Bisipara's status system, I could not have been a jajman. A haircut from Sugri, the younger of Bisipara's two Barbers, at that time cost me four annas. (The village, probably in the person of the sirdar, had determined that I should patronize Sugri, rather than his uncle. I was not consulted.) Every week in Phulbani market there is a line of Barbers ready to cut hair or shave a man for cash. They can also be hired to do the work needed at a funeral or a wedding or any other ritual occasion, public or private. The same was true of the other specialist castes, including the Washerman. Only untouchables would not be able to hire specialists, since any such person who provided an untouchable household with these status-giving services would be outcaste by his own samaj and boycotted by everyone else.

Reflecting on this framework one has a clearer notion both of Tuta's marginal position in Bisipara and of the structure that made him marginal. Bisipara's universe revolved around its one-time lords, the Bisois. The Bisois were like a sun. They stood alone at the center. They had a mythology of the places where their ancestors had lived, and in a few instances they could name villages where agnates (those related by descent through males) still lived. But these places were mostly distant, and the connections had no present-day social importance. The Bisois did, however, have extensive ties of kinship with people in other Oriya villages in the Kondmals, but these were all through women who had come to marry Bisipara men or who had gone from Bisipara to marry men in other villages. In that respect the village was like an entrepot of Warrior men, descended through males from a common male ancestor, who carried on through the generations a continuing trade in women with groups like themselves. Around this central core of Bisois in Bisipara clustered a few households of other Warriors, all related to the Bisois by ties through a woman. The household of Madhia Behera, the jati puo for Jodu's faction, and a household bearing the family name of Naik, who did the same job for the sirdar's party, are examples.

Once upon a time the Bisois (and attached families such as Madhia's) owned all the land, and land was the sole source of wealth. That is how people in Bisipara saw their past. People in other castes, following their dharma, made their living by working for Warriors, as one or another kind of specialist or, in the case of the Panos, as farm laborers. This work, whether everyday technical stuff needed to grow crops or the ritual work required to ensure prosperity and good health, was essential for the continuation of the community; nevertheless it marked the village servants as secondary members of the community. The community needed them, but they were not regarded as part of its essence. (In that respect their position resembled that of in-marrying women.)

The reality of this situation is mostly gone, blown away by the winds of change that came a century earlier with the Meriah Wars and imperialism and a changing economy. In 1953 those with the largest per capita landholding were Gumsur Distillers, not Warriors. There were Warriors who had no land. There were Panos (a few) who owned many fields. Land was no longer the only source of wealth; people could support themselves, sometimes becoming rich, in commerce or working for the administration. But "the tradition of all the dead generations weighs like a nightmare on the brain of the living," to quote a purple patch from Karl Marx, and in Bisipara in 1953 the Warriors and most other castes (when it suited them) continued to show respect for a tradition that was no longer in fact a reality. They behaved as if the village was still a closed community and tried to ignore the ways in which individuals (or sometimes groups) could pursue their own interests and defy community values. Whenever possible, its former rulers sought to preserve the ideal village by marginalizing or expelling those who did not conform to the old pattern. This tendency was clearly manifested in the continuing paranoid apprehension that those whom they marginalized would resort to the courts.

Even before the alien government took control of the region and brought new opportunities to Bisipara's underlings, an opposition must have existed between the solid corporate body that is the community and the individualized parts that make it up. That tension is a feature of every collectivity. Bisipara's undivided entity is notionally the core of agnatic male kinsmen, the Bisois themselves. But even within that group each household, indeed, each married male, is individuated by virtue of connections with other villages through marriage. Each woman is a fault line in the crust of male solidarity. Men have no doubt that this is the case. When a woman is left a widow, she has the right to live off her late husband's lands, perhaps working them through a sharecropping arrangement. Even if she has no children, she still has this right. But she has it only as a trustee. She may not sell the land, and when she dies or leaves the village the land reverts to a male of her husband's lineage. The men of that lineage watch jealously to see that none of their patrimony is given away to the woman's own male kin. Rarely do they extend themselves to help the widow. One such woman, the widow of a Bisoi, with a small son and two daughters, and very poor, found no help from her late husband's kin, and would have had her house fall in around her had her father and brothers not come to Bisipara to rebuild it. In such a setting a woman who does not have a son of her own is inevitably suspect. This is another aspect of the same mistrust that is manifested in the blame conventionally heaped on the in-marrying woman for causing dissension in the patriarchal joint family. Men cannot marry their sisters, and so the stranger woman is brought into the group, needed for the group to continue through the generations, but, as the men see it, she always remains a threat to its solidarity.

The specialist castes repeat this pattern. The corporate group needs them, but they too are strangers, externalized by their special skills, by their relative mobility and their links with other villages, and by not having a (traditional) stake in the land. Modernity—new ways of making a living that do not depend on subservience to a group of Warriors, the rule of law that more or less removed the Warriors' ability to rule by the use of force, and the ever-encroaching world of commerce—has fastened on these traditional lines of cleavage and intensified them. That is the background to the witch-hunt that finally caused Tuta to get up and run away in the middle of the night. But it is not, as will become clear, a complete explanation for what was done at that time in Bisipara. What I have described is the structure within which people made their tactical moves in pursuit of their own advantage.

Tuta did not stay away long. His wife and children had remained in Bisipara. He had a regular arrangement to sharecrop fields there, not a large estate, but, by village standards, certainly giving him more than a trivial income. He was one of those twenty-five or thirty householders who could afford to lend out paddy, and he had a number of loans outstanding at the time. He also, I heard, had a side business as a moneylender; and he was still at least partly functioning, despite the present hullabaloo, as Bisipara's Washerman. These were strong incentives for him not to abandon Bisipara and settle in another place, as his brother had done ten years earlier. In fact, when he came back on April 8 (two days after the Ramnobomi festivities ended), he gave out that he had gone away only in order to find expert help to rid him of the troublesome devata that, despite his wishes, evidently continued to hang around his house.

The rumor went around—it came to me from Debohari—that Tuta had brought back various objects that would, like flypaper, attract the devata. Tuta could then carry out the objects and the trapped devata and dispose of them in a suitable place. "He got the stuff," Debohari said, "from some Harijan." Debohari was skeptical, adding that they would want a lot of people standing by and watching before they believed that Tuta was really doing anything effective. I noted Debohari's use of "Harijan." This title, given to untouchables by Gandhi, means "children of God." For Bisipara Warriors and the other clean castes *Harijan* had become a term of opprobrium, for it was used by their own fractious Boad Panos to claim a freedom that tradition did not give them but the government had decided was their due. I was surprised that Debohari should volunteer the gunia's caste—previously I had to prompt for it—for men, while they acted in that capacity, were notionally outside the caste system, just as Bhuani was. On that occasion I think he was using the word, racist fashion, to devalue the product and to belittle Tuta's efforts. I heard no more about Tuta's flypaper magic.

The panchayat met in the mandap on the night of Thursday April 9. Tuta was present and, according to Debohari, he said that while he was away he had traveled about and made contact with two people who worked together as gunias. They had a very good reputation and were willing to come to Bisipara, but would not come just on his invitation. He, Tuta, requested the village to invite them. Everyone "indignantly refused" (this is still Debohari's account), saying they would decide on a gunia for themselves, and, when they had found one, Tuta would pay sixty rupees toward the cost. If he refused, the village would boycott him. Next day they would all swear an oath before Sri Ramchandro that they would all join in expelling from the village anyone found harboring a malevolent devata, if he or she refused to do what was necessary to make things right again. This was the consensus announced by the sirdar. Tuta began to protest that he was a poor man and could not afford to pay that much. Thereupon Susila's father and several other people shouted at him: "You brought it! You pay to get rid of it!" The meeting went on to appoint four men to go and inquire in other villages where there might be gunias capable of doing what was needed. They further assessed each household at one rupee to meet general expenses. The other four offenders would each pay four rupees.

They met again next morning, this time in the street in front of Sri Ramchandro's temple. The canopy that had been built for Ramnobomi—a wood frame like a pergola, six or seven feet high loosely roofed with leafy branches—still stood, and the older men crowded in its shade, leaving younger men on the margins. In the mandap, which had a smooth mud-plastered floor and an ample supply of mats, men sat in a rough circle, cross-legged or in a lotus position or with their legs stretched straight before them. But the street was dusty and there were no mats. There the men squatted in rows, all facing the temple, like people on a bus, each man neatly and compactly parceled, legs so perfectly bent at knee and hip that back and shin were parallel. Bisipara people find it restful to sit so, backsides tucked in hard against the heels, and one can hear old men and old women sigh with satisfaction when they fold themselves in that way, after standing or walking. They use the same posture to work at tasks that for us require a table and chair or a workbench. They prepare food, resting on their heels, and they use that position when they cook over a fire. Carpenters squat, sometimes holding the wood steady with their feet. Jodu the postmaster had a small sloping table eight inches high that served as his writing desk, and he wrote out receipts and kept his daily accounts squatting behind it or sometimes sitting lotus fashion.

The decisions made at the meeting the previous night were repeated: one rupee per house, four rupees for the four offenders, and sixty rupees for the fifth, Tuta. Someone—I did not notice who it was—suggested they should see how much money the rupee-per-house collection brought in, and then make Tuta match that amount. There was an argument about the rights and wrongs of this, most of it being assertions that this was not the usual way of assessing a penalty. My uncharitable guess is that running through some people's minds was a calculation about whether this would cause Tuta to pay more or less than sixty rupees. No one was crass enough to say so plainly. In the end they settled for sixty and agreed that any money remaining after the divination would be placed in Sri Ramchandro's fund.

I never managed to find out how they arrived at the figure sixty or what arguments they used to justify it. They had shifted from an original seven rupees, one week's wages for a laborer, to the equivalent of two month's wages. The gap between what Tuta would pay and what the other offenders would pay had gone from roughly twice to fifteen times as much. At least in Tuta's case, it seemed that the collegial anxiety to get village affairs back on track was now subordinated to an attitude that better fits the spirit of our own legal system when it sets out to punish offenders "with the full rigor of the law." I could not work out what notion they had of justice. With regard to the offense itself, keeping a devata, nothing significant had changed since the evening of March 21 when they fixed Tuta's penalty at seven rupees. Admittedly, Sadhu's wife had thrown a fit, with maximum dramatic effect but no obvious harm, and had confirmed the verdict of Bhuani (which, of course, Sadhu's wife knew about already). Her seizure also revealed that the devata had not been properly expelled. But was that Tuta's fault? Or the dehuri's who conducted the divination? I entertained myself with the idea that the panchayat should ask for its five rupees back from the man in Dangolu, until I remembered that we do not ask for our money back when the doctor fails to cure lower-back pain.

Then I thought perhaps I might be witnessing some kind of vindictive panic, a crowd in pursuit of a victim. If that feeling was around, it would explain why Tuta ran away. But then he had come back after a few days. I was left with the thought that strings were being pulled and that Sadhu's wife's hysteria was more a convenient occasion than a reason for turning the screws so hard on Tuta. The figure sixty was not related at all to the cost of the divination and cleansing; it probably represented someone's guess about how much Tuta could be made to bleed.

Almost as soon as they had settled on sixty rupees, a violent argument broke out between Sripati (the man who had informed on his brother) and Kopilo, who was renowned for having a short fuse. They spoke so fast and, in Kopilo's case, with such fury, that I could not gather what the argument was about, especially when they both began to shout at the same time and other people joined in. This was not the way people usually conducted themselves at panchayat meetings. I gathered later that Sripati had been trying to get his brother Bagoboto, who was not present, out of having to pay the one rupee in addition to the four required of him as an offender. (Other things were lost to me in this brouhaha, as I later discovered.)

Bagoboto was absent, but his wife had walked the half-mile from where they lived and she sat on her heels across the street, within hearing range but conspicuously not part of the panchayat. Beside her was the spinster Srimati, one of the offenders. Near them, also squatting in the dust, was Chanti's husband and his elder brother's adult son. As untouchables they could not be members of the panchayat, but they had come to hear what was going on. The elder brother had himself died on February 17 that year, about a month before Susila, in circumstances that might in a different person have indicated possession by a devata. He had taken a fever when visiting his wife's people; they carried him back on a charpoy but he died, delirious, the next day. He was in his fifties and an untouchable, and I heard nothing said about devatas.

Untouchables like Chanti's husband and all the Panos were excluded from the panchayat and did not take part in its debates. Neither did women. Their exclusion was explained to me as necessary because the panchayat usually met in the mandap, which was a sacred building that would be polluted by the presence of women or untouchables. But I noticed that women entered the mandap, when there was no meeting going on, to replaster worn places in the floor. I also noticed that when the panchayat met elsewhere (a favorite place being the shade of a full-grown banyan tree near the bungalow) the members formed a compact cluster, while others—untouchables or sometimes women—sat well apart. Evidently the body of men carried its sacredness around with it.

Out under the tree or in the street, the same rules applied; nonmembers were allowed to speak only when invited to do so. The panchayat sometimes functioned as a judicial body, hearing disputes and complaints and seeking to find a way of resolving them. Since people disqualified from panchayat membership often got into that kind of trouble, the device of the external meeting allowed them to attend and to give evidence and state their cases in a setting more convenient than the mandap. The sirdar heard cases from his Konds in this way; they would come in from their own villages, some of them several hours walk away, to have disputes arbitrated. (The presence of Konds would not have polluted the mandap, but they often came in numbers too large to make it a convenient place for the hearing.) Marital disputes, including some within Pano households, could be adjudicated by the panchayat. If the cases were particularly difficult, or if they involved some issue peculiar to the caste, the village panchayat might suggest to the disputants that they take the case to the elders of their own caste samaj.

When the quarrel in the panchayat between Kopilo and Sripati subsided, Bagoboto's wife started up. She stood up and began to hector the men, talking down from above them. She had a loud and penetrating voice, and she kept repeating that her husband had done no wrong and neither had the spinster Srimati and that they were poor people. She said this over and over again, seeming to be stuck in a rhetorical loop. The men, now debating in a more restrained fashion, soon found this harangue intolerable, and the sirdar rose to his feet and spoke sternly, telling her to be quiet or take herself away. A woman could listen, he said, but it was not right for her to speak unless they invited her to say something. The two women stayed where they were, Bagoboto's wife eventually squatting down to go on listening and watching. She did not raise her voice again.

When the loud arguments had stopped, men began coming forward and handing over a rupee. Suren had brought a mat and was lying on his stomach writing the names of those who paid up. While this was going on, people were looking around and noticing who was not present, and then one of the younger men would be sent off to find the absentee and bring him to the meeting. When he arrived, someone would explain, almost in the manner of a clerk reading out a proclamation, that it was the will of all the people in the village that every house should contribute a rupee to pay for another divination. Different people played this role; I could not work out how they selected themselves. The person would then return to his house and go to the hiding place where he kept his cash and bring back a rupee, which Suren duly recorded. As a way of doing business, it was both leisurely and somewhat hit-and-miss. They did not consult a list or a register, although I know that Suren owned a house-by-house list of voters in Bisipara. (He had been a temporary clerk when the electoral register was compiled in 1951.) Messengers would go to a house in one street and summon the occupant; then five minutes later someone would notice that the man living two doors away in the same street had not paid up, and back a messenger would go.

Chano Mehera, the man who had built the temple in Hatopodera, sat at the meeting along with another old man, also poor. People began shouting to them to go and get their rupees, but they just sat there. "You know what will happen. You won't be able to remain in the village. Go on! Get the money!" The tone, despite the words, was not unfriendly; almost pleading, at times cajoling, the tone that people use to address the slightly senile. Chano did not pay up, certainly not then, and probably not later either; the threats were empty, and no one intended that he should be driven from the village.

Chano had been a rich man. He came to Bisipara many years earlier, the story goes, from a place called Bhagvali, carrying nothing but "a mat and a pot." He took goods on credit from a shopkeeper in Hatopodera and made a living hawking them around Kond villages. He prospered, but not excessively. Then one day, building an extra room on his house, he unearthed a brass pot full of gold coins. It had been buried there by a man, long since dead, who had been a moneylender. Chano himself set up a moneylending business and acquired land from people who defaulted on their loans. He traded, he kept a shop, and eventually he grew so wealthy that he began to feel uneasy. Having all that wealth, he must do something to earn spiritual merit.

There are many ways of doing this in Hinduism, notable among them being to give gifts to Brahmins. That was not the way in Bisipara; the local Brahmins, familiar faces, came in for a good deal of contempt. Some good works that qualify for spiritual merit can be quite minor, for example planting a tree that one day will provide shade. Someone had built three small rooms on the track that ran near Hatopodera, as places where weary travelers might rest. In a neighboring village a rich Kond, two generations back, an unscrupulous man who had used his good connections with administrators to cheat many of his fellow villagers out of their land, in old age constructed an enormous pond (in India called a tank) complete with concrete steps so that people might conveniently take their baths there. He had done so because he had no son, despite having two wives. Then a son was born. But the father had accumulated so many demerits, people said, that even the tank was not enough, and the old man lived to see his son die, still a young man, still unmarried.

Such public benefactions are often the outcome of a vow, a man's promising to excavate a tank or build a temple or make an offering at a shrine, if some boon is granted to him—the birth of a son, a recovery from illness, and the like. Bagoboto, in May 1953, dedicated a regal umbrella to Sri Ramchandro, having made a pledge seven years earlier in the hope that a daughter would be born to his wife. The girl was now six years old. Perhaps he thought that by then she had a secure hold on life. Perhaps also he was moved to fulfill his vow so as to improve his image after the recent troubles over his devata. (He died the following year, and I have a note of the panchayat's commending him for the many good services he had done for the community.)

A temple is no small undertaking. I do not know why Chano built his, whether to fulfill a vow or simply to cancel out some of the spiritual demerits that inevitably, in Bisipara reasoning, are accumulated by those who amass spectacular riches. No virtuous person can become rich above his station in life. Chano was a Weaver, a caste that in Bisipara is not untouchable but does have low status. As in the case of the rich Kond, Chano must have been overburdened with sin. Rumor has it that his troubles began when he thrashed an ox so badly that it died. He became ill and spent much money on various treatments. Then his wife fell ill and died. Another ox died. Experts advised him that the deity he had installed in his temple in Hatopodera was discontented, and, following their advice, he had the expense of transferring it to a temple in Puri, more than a hundred miles away on the coast of Orissa. For that he paid two hundred rupees.

In that way his fortune was lost. He took to ganja (marijuana). He had one son, not yet married, who had turned out to be a wastrel and a spendthrift (but a much-admired performer on the mrudungo). He lived with this son, who occasionally worked at a loom to eke out the living that they got from the few fields remaining in their possession. Chano was an emaciated old man, his body crooked toward the long stick that he used to help him walk. Much of the time he seemed to be in a daze. But children did not tease him, as they did some other old people, perhaps because they could not get a rise out of him. People spoke of him mostly with compassion. Debohari, who sometimes was given to moralizing, pointed him out to me as a tragic example of what will happen to those who single-mindedly (and successfully) seek after riches.

In that respect Chano was a walking parable for the people of Bisipara. Everyone knew his story and no doubt derived some satisfaction from contemplating a mighty fall. Everyone knew him, although in 1953 he was rarely in a condition to take part even in a conversation. In fact, in Bisipara every adult knew, or at least knew of, almost everyone else. When the time came to take my own census, I did not go from house to house, walking through the village. I sat in the bungalow with one or two of the people who helped me—Jaya, Kopilo, Debohari, and others—and we followed the map that Debohari had drawn of all the courtyards and the houses in them, and listed the occupants. Only for the old Panosai did this method fail with those informants. They knew roughly where the houses were and the names of the men; they knew the names of old women ("So-and-so's mother") and often the names of the villages from which they had come to marry Bisipara men; they knew about wives, but often could not name them, and had only the haziest ideas about small children. Sindhu the schoolmaster, a Pano, filled out the list for me. (I suppose he would not have known about clean-caste households; I did not ask.) The list was accurate. Later Suren produced his handwritten register of eligible voters, compiled for the 1952 election; my census matched. Moreover, after two years of casual encounters in the village, and after collecting genealogies that covered everyone in the village, all the time cross-listing with the census, I uncovered no more than a few inaccuracies. There is a formidably large amount of shared taken-for-granted people-knowledge on tap in places like Bisipara.

The listing took a long time because there were stories to be told about some of those named, and casual bits of information

were volunteered, allowing me to see how they mapped their
social world. I didn't ask in the census for the places from which
wives and mothers had come (I did in the genealogies, which
mostly were gathered later), but my helpers seemed to have a
sense of incompleteness if they did not give me that information.
Evidently, where she came from was part of a woman's identity.
Sometimes, stymied for the moment over the place of origin of
someone's old mother, Debohari or Jaya or Romesh might say,
"Good! Now I remember. She is Dhoni's mother's brother's house
(*mamughoro*). She comes from Gumagarh." We might have been
talking about a person of some caste other than the speaker, even
a Pano; they could not have been related by blood. The point is
that Dhoni's mother came from Gumagarh; therefore all people
in that village, whatever their caste, rated as, and the adult males
would be addressed by Dhoni as, mother's brothers. From this
perspective Bisipara was like the hub on a map of airline routes,
with hundreds and hundreds of mamughoro spokes (not to men-
tion lines through wives and sisters) binding it to all the other
Oriya villages in the Kondmals.

There were some gaps in this gigantic repertoire of tacit knowledge about persons (*tacit* in the sense that it was knowledge
never formally taught but assimilated, knowledge they hardly
knew they had until they came to use it). One mystery was the
place of Srimati the spinster, who on that morning was about
to pay up the four rupees the panchayat demanded. She lived
in Hatopodera, where in the past a weekly market had been
held. (Bisipara was the administrative capital of the Kondmals
from about 1855 until 1904, when the government moved itself
to Phulbani.) Srimati owned some land, which she rented out
to sharecroppers. I was told that she lent out money and grain
and was probably wealthier than she appeared to be. I think her
caste was now the same as that of Chano the Weaver. Her sister, by then dead, had lived in the house next to Srimati's and
had married into a Weaver family in Hatopodera. That marriage
produced a boy, now about seventeen, who lived with Srimati,
his father having married again. The mystery was that Srimati

and her sister were listed as having been born in Bisipara, but they did not appear in any Weaver genealogy. I think their caste was Oilman. No Oilman families lived in Bisipara at the time I knew it. The Weaver family into which the sister had married had several peculiar unions; in particular a brother of Srimati's late sister's husband had disgraced himself by marrying a Pano wife and had gone away from Bisipara to live elsewhere. The following year, in April, the young nephew married a girl of mixed parentage. It also seems likely—I never followed up the hints— that Srimati had shared her sister's Weaver husband. The vote list gave her age as thirty-two; she looked older. She died in June the following year.

For the most part I was not made privy to sexual scandals in the village, until they erupted into the public domain. The escapades of Ganesa's priapic brother were well known. Kopilo had his middle-age fling with Rua, the widow. In 1953 an unmarried Potter girl had a child by a Distiller. The previous year another Potter, also unmarried, was made pregnant by a Writer, a man from the plains, temporarily employed in the shop in Warrior street—the same man who so astonished the panchayat by his short-lived open defiance. She had a daughter, but the child—my informant was not quite callous enough to say "fortunately"— died. For a time some other Potters made a half-hearted attempt to boycott the girl and her household, but things soon went back to normal. A more bizarre case was that of Durja Malik. His father was a Potter working as a servant in the Brahmin household to which Ganesa belonged. The servant impregnated Ganesa's widowed aunt. She died soon afterward; so did the servant. Durja was brought up by a woman who was the Potter widow of a Muslim and lived in Hatopodera. The pair of them seemed to be accepted, somewhat marginally, as Potters.

A major scandal was created by the rich Christian widow's eccentric stepson, the man who had shot the bull. In 1953 he made pregnant a Kond girl (about eighteen years old) who was a servant in his house. That was the second occasion; the first child, born two years earlier, died soon after birth. This time the affair became public because the unfortunate girl threw the new-born child down the well in the street of the Warriors. (It may have been stillborn.) They drained the well and chlorinated it so thoroughly that it had to be drained again, and the water was still undrinkable after two weeks.

A somewhat unbalanced old Sweeper woman—Chanti's moth-er-in-law—had acted as midwife. Chanti's husband, hearing from his mother what had happened, went to look in the well and then alerted the sirdar, who sent for the police. The tale told them was that the Kond girl had thrown the child in the well because its father ordered her to do so. His story was that he had been told the child was stillborn and he simply sent a message to dispose of it. I saw the police interrogate the midwife, her twelve-year-old granddaughter (alleged to have been present), and the Kond girl. The questions were accompanied by some violence until the senior policeman gestured toward me, and the slapping stopped. Other people were questioned, and they all resolutely insisted they had noticed nothing at all, not even the servant girl's preg-nant condition. This interrogation took place on March 15, three days before Susila died.

The following day the deputy superintendent of police came to Bisipara. His presence put everyone in mortal terror, and, it was said, when the Christian man was questioned, he promptly fainted. There would surely be a court case against the man, they said in the village, but they did not know what the charge would be. I knew him slightly, and later on the day of his interrogation he came to visit me (he had a headache and wanted aspirin). He acknowledged his accident (his word), but blamed the foolish old Sweeper woman for what had been done and claimed that the sirdar had prompted her to put the blame on him. He was arrested and spent a short time in jail. Oruno (the old man's step-mother's Brahmin grandson) proudly told everyone that he had seen the arrest coming, when he cast his uncle's horoscope. The uncle's influential family bailed him out, and he was tried eight months later, and acquitted. At that time the Kond girl was still in jail, awaiting trial. She was released in July 1954. She did not return to Bisipara, and I do not know what became of her.

Up front the attitude toward sexual adventuring was quite Victorian. In February 1955 the sirdar went out one night to ease himself at the end of his garden. Hearing a noise coming from the adjoining house he looked over the fence. He could see nothing, but he heard the voices of several youths coming from a part of the house that was occupied by a young widow. Shocked, he took himself to the mandap and there, instead of the dozen or so young men that he expected to find sleeping, he found only three. It was after midnight. Next day he called a meeting, the record of which was written for me by Debohari. How much Debohari's sententiousness contributed to it, I cannot tell, but it is a pleasing example of Ciceronian outrage: "Oh! The morals of our day!" (*O tempora, O mores!*) A stern warning was delivered to the young people of the village. Women were told to keep a close watch over the girls. Sometimes girls from Pano street, Debohari wrote, deliberately let a breast hang out to excite respectable boys. The boys were enjoined to take no notice and never to respond to flirtatious remarks. Youths should work hard and not hang about. "The adults spoke at considerable length on this subject and the youths received copious advice. It was remarked that nowadays youths do not listen to what their elders tell them." Women were told not to take their bath in the river near the ford; too many people could pass that way. Men were forbidden to defecate on a bluff that overlooked the women's bathing place. (It was considered good manners, approaching the river on a sunken path that led by a place where women bathed, for a man to shout "Who's having a bath there? Put your clothes on!" and to pause for a moment to let the women do so.)

Sustained liaisons across caste (as distinct from casual fornication), if they came to public notice and were confirmed or acknowledged, automatically reduced the couple to whichever caste was lower. Kopilo's father, a Herdsman, had come from Gumsur to Bisipara some time in the last decades of the nineteenth century. He was a policeman. He took as wife a Brahmin girl, a distant relative of that formidable old Brahmin lady who had married a Christian. Kopilo, as a young man, had regularized his status with the local Herdsmen by sponsoring a feast for them and had married a Herdsman girl from Bisipara (Rua's sister-in-law). I stumbled onto other cases through genealogies, by finding, for example, a typically Potter surname in a family acknowledged to be Pano. It was explained that the father or the grandfather had crossed the line. As in the case of Kopilo's peccadillo (his affair with Rua, not his ancestry, in which he took a mild pride), matters of this kind seem to be buried away in the public memory, until someone found a use for them. After two or three generations, however, all but a few of them must be forgotten.

In Bisipara, both Distillers and Weavers were associated with commerce, for which there was, among the traditional landowning caste, the Warriors, a lingering disfavor (although they themselves lost no opportunity to trade for turmeric). For years the Konds refused to be middlemen, much to their own disadvantage, for they allowed Panos and Oriyas from places such as Bisipara (and their own Kond Panos) to insert themselves as middlemen in the turmeric trade. Indeed, nineteenth-century accounts of the Kondmals speak of a village official called "Digaloo," glossed as "interpreter." Digalo was a common lineage name among Kond Panos, and the Digaloo was no more than someone put forward by the Konds to spare them contact with outsiders.

Warriors went enthusiastically into turmeric trading, the sirdar making use of his influence to monopolize some of the best suppliers in the area. At the meeting on April 9, when notice of the oath to be taken next day was given, the leading men uttered a stern warning that people must show up and should not go off trading for turmeric. But shopkeeping was not in the Warrior line; nor did they look with admiration on careers like that of their own Basu Pradhan, the Distiller who made a lot of money out of commerce and taking government contracts. In 1953 land was still the only unambiguously respectable foundation for wealth. Earlier in the century, the many Distillers who became wealthy through their monopoly of liquor licenses invested their profits in land. For that reason Hatopodera—the place of traders and shopkeepers, where wealth did not reside in land—stood at the margins of the village community. To a degree, the people who resided there, like Srimati the spinster, represented values that were contrary to the core values of the landowning community; the situation parallels the contrasting values in Phulbani between its Hatopodera and the orderliness of the government lines. Srimati—another name for Radha, the mistress of Krishna—thus qualified in several ways as a marginal person in Bisipara.

When they had collected as many subscriptions as they thought they would get and had stopped sending out messengers to bring in the absentees, they all got to their feet and stood facing the door of the temple. The young Brahmin Ganesa went inside and brought out a stool on which he placed a palm-leaf book. Then he stood behind it and recited an oath, to which everyone listened with their hands held together before them, as we do in prayer. Ganesa was evidently out of his depth; Oruno stood beside him, prompting almost every word. Then another man, Rotona, one of the Bisipara Potters, came to the front and shouted some words. His voice was harsh and unmelodious, quite unlike the gentle almost musical intonation of the Brahmins. Everyone cried out "*Haribolo!*", invoking God to witness what had just been done. I did not understand a word, neither of Ganesa nor of Rotona, but I realized that I had witnessed the promised oath before Sri Ramchandro; they had sworn to expel from the village anyone who kept a malignant devata and refused to accept the panchayat's punishment for doing so. This, I concluded, was the reason why the panchayat met in the street in front of Sri Ramchandro's temple instead of in their usual place, the mandap.

Somewhere in that meeting, probably in its tumultuous beginning, I had failed to notice that plans for the divination had been changed. The previous night they had appointed a search committee to travel around other villages and find the right gunia for the job; they had even assessed each household at a half-pint measure of rice, so that the travelers could be provisioned. The latest decision was that the divination would be conducted by one of their own gunias, Rotona.

A boastful man, Rotona announced, as the meeting concluded, that if he did not succeed in expelling the devatas, he "would not drink the water of Bisipara again." They did not hold him to his promise.

Winding Down

The panchayat met again that same evening, April 10, this time in the mandap. Three meetings in twenty-four hours should indicate a sense of urgency, but if they were anxious to bring matters to completion, the anxiety was not at first apparent. They sat around, waiting for people to turn up. Someone would remark that so-and-so was not here, and there would be some rambling talk about whether he had gone visiting, and, if so, where, and then one of the younger men would be sent off to fetch him. Meetings were not scheduled for a particular hour, it being generally understood that after the sun had set and people had finished their meal—this was the hot weather when the main meal was eaten after dark—the tocsin (the empty kerosene tin) would be sounded and, hearing it, people would come and the meeting would get under way. No one in Bisipara in 1953 had a watch that worked. Some people, when they heard the summons, were still eating and they took their time, so that meetings were slow to start. Occasionally they fretted about punctuality. In October that year they started imposing one-anna fines for not turning up in good time. (The money, they said, would be used to buy kerosine for the single storm lantern that shed its meager light on nighttime meetings.) But, without a timepiece and still more without the mentality that goes with clocks, it was hard to know where to draw the line, and the rule was soon forgotten. In any case, sending for people was easy enough. Except for those who lived in New street (Bagoboto and Sripati and eight or nine other men) no one had more than three hundred yards to walk to reach the mandap.

From time to time Chano would be urged to go and get his rupee, but he sat there, saying nothing, as he had done earlier in the day. I think they were teasing him, amusing themselves, killing time while they waited. The other old man who had not paid up did not come to this meeting, but, someone said, he had promised that his brother would be bringing the rupee. The brother did not show up.

I had a stock of Paludrine tablets that I wanted to make available through Syamo, Susila's father, who dispensed herbal medicines. They talked about that for a time, but they seemed to be skirting round the decision I wanted them to make, and nothing conclusive was arranged. I suspected they were reluctant, then and later, to let any one of them, even Susila's father, who was a respected and noncontentious figure, gain control of something new and unfamiliar. They preferred to leave matters in the hands of the outsider, me. They did not say so directly, only that they would talk some more about the best way to do things. They seemed to me irrationally cautious about innovations that might even slightly change the existing pattern of power relations. Everyone was cautious when faced with something new, including those who had no power to lose anyway.

Then one of the Bisois, Doya, a younger paternal cousin of the sirdar and living in the same courtyard, an assertive go-getting man who worked for the local agent of the company that collected leaves for bidi cigarettes, suddenly turned on Tuta and said, "Go and get it!" Tuta hesitated as if he were about to argue. Doya, speaking in a tone and with an expression that surprised me by its sudden violent rage, repeated the order. It did surprise me, and I never found out why Doya was so immediately incensed. I had not seen him behave that way before, although he was a bumptious fellow, always ready enough to order people about. The usual Bisipara manner for dealing with inferiors is one of effortless superiority, an unemotional monosyllabic indifference, as if talking to a thing or an animal. No one else spoke, and nothing more was said while Tuta limped away home and came back a few minutes later with a gamucha knotted into a bundle. He put it on the ground by the sirdar, and Doya came forward, opened the bundle, and, one by one and aloud, counted sixty rupees. It was a performance; he conducted himself as one uplifted by the triumph of morality, enumerating one by one the tokens of justice done, gloating, anything but sad-eyed. It seemed a pity that the herald of the collectivity's restored integrity should have been such a mean-spirited man.

When the counting had finished, the mood changed abruptly. Perhaps they were a little embarrassed, as I was, by Doya's performance; perhaps not, for I had seen this abrupt change of collective countenance before. They behaved like an audience in a theater when the curtain comes down on an act; this was an intermission. There was no longer a center of attention, and they started chattering to one another. I noticed Suren writing in his ledger, presumably entering Tuta's sixty rupees. I had seen other collective performances in Bisipara punctuated in that way. Out hunting in the hot weather, they would pause between beats and sit around talking idly about the deer or the peacock that doubled back through the line of beaters or about where they should try next. When they were working later in the year to clear boulders from a watercourse that would feed into one of the main irrigation channels, they toiled frantically for five or ten minutes and then, in an unspoken consensus, they would all sit on their heels, gamuchas draped over their heads and sweat-stained shoulders, contemplating the work and grumbling about those who had not turned up. Work started again, with people standing and stretching and urging one another to go to it. Panchayat meetings ran more or less the same way. After an intermission they would shepherd each other back toward the agenda.

The next task was to make the arrangements for the following day's divination. The discussion seemed to me to be on the level of detailed triviality; it was distinctly unhurried. They asked

Rotona what he would need. First he requested four coconuts. Coconuts could be bought from the *sahukar* (the store at the end of Warrior street), someone said, and there followed a leisurely discussion about how much should be paid for them. The amount was very small, but they took their time making a decision, and then money was handed over to someone who was to buy the coconuts next morning. Suren duly made an entry in his ledger. Next Rotona said he would need milk. Two annas were given to a young man to go to a nearby Kond village where it was known that someone had a cow that was lactating. Cows are not well fed and are hard worked, often yoked to pull a plow, and, when lactating, seem to produce about a pint of milk at a time. Milk is scarce, and in their tea Bisipara people always use the powdered stuff. Then another man was given two rupees and four annas to buy some orua rice and a bottle of liquor and various other things. (*Orua caulo* is rice from paddy that has not been boiled before husking. It is used to grind into flour and is mandatory for rituals. *Usna caulo* is made from paddy that has been boiled before husking and is the preferred form for bhato, rice cooked and ready for eating. The boiling, which slightly discolors the rice, also transfers vitamin B_1 from the husk into the grain and protects the eater from beriberi.) Business moved slowly because, for each item, they pooled their collective wisdom and argued back and forth about where to find it and how much to pay for it. Then someone had second thoughts about the milk and suggested that the cow might have dried up, but he knew a place where they could, for sure, get buffalo milk. Rotona was asked if he could manage with buffalo milk. He took some time to think about it and then said, apologetically, that no, it would have to be cow's milk. They went on arguing about when the cow had calved and whether they could reasonably expect to get a glassful of milk out of it. Tuta sat there, saying nothing.

The problem with the milk drifted off the agenda, and they were now telling each other that next day everyone really must be in attendance, and it would be a very bad thing for anyone to duck the meeting and go off trading for turmeric. The leading men took turns to utter the same stern warning in more or less the same words. They had a liking for sententious repetition, as if believing that anything said solemnly and often enough would become a reality.

My mind was wandering away to a book I had read about the tendency of committees to become obsessive over details, when I realized that the topic had shifted again. They were talking about selecting four youths who would be needed for the divination next day. They went through several names and then decided to postpone the choice until next morning.

The last thing they did, before the meeting broke up and they all went home, was entrust fifty rupees in coins to one of the Kond Potters (Ramo Kohoro, another man with a polio limp). His job was to change the coins for notes of larger denomination and then deposit these with Jodu in the post office. Coins-into-notes makes sense, because four annas or even a rupee more easily disappear than does a ten-rupee note. At least it makes sense until one remembers that the money was to be deposited in the post office. The logical course would have been to bank the cash in a savings account, but my memory is that Jodu's branch post office did not provide facilities for that. I guess they wanted the money put in the large Godrej steel box that served Jodu for a safe—he processed registered mail and money orders and, of course, he had to handle cash.

Jodu's post office (a room off his courtyard that had a barred window and a solid door that could be padlocked) did exhibit, within its very limited scope, a rocklike reliability. It had been opened five years earlier and was officially designated "experimental." In 1954 the postal service announced that the office would be closed because it did not do a sufficient volume of business. The panchayat petitioned for it to remain open. When the postal authorities offered to do so if the village made good the loss, the villagers, with a logic that they found very satisfying, responded by asking whether, if the post office had made a profit in its first five years, the money would have gone to Bisipara. The village won the issue (probably not with that particular argument), and the post office was still open when I returned to Bisipara in 1959.

Each working day (five in a week) Jodu wrote up his accounts, sealed the mail in a canvas bag, cycled two miles to the road junction to wait for the bus, deposited his sack with the conductor and collected the incoming mail, cycled back to Bisipara, and in his own good time distributed the mail to whoever was on hand and might be going near the house of the addressee. Sending out a parcel or registered mail, or even buying stamps for a letter, usually took half an hour, or even longer; nothing ever seemed to be done in a hurry. But it was an efficient institution; so far as I know, in two years nothing of ours, incoming or outgoing, ever went astray (including the small fortune, by village standards, that the bank in Cuttack transmitted to us each month).

I still have no sure idea why they could not have handed the fifty rupees straight over to Jodu, who was present at the meeting. Perhaps they were playing the perpetual game of omnidirectional mistrust. I thought of a comment Jodu made to me. Debohari had recently arranged to send his younger sister in marriage to Gumagarh and had already received sixty-five rupees in bridewealth. Then the sirdar intervened and vetoed the marriage on the grounds that there were too many kin connections with that family already. Debohari had to return the bridewealth, and he did so in the form of a money order. It was very smart of him, Jodu remarked, for in that way he would not need to assemble a posse of witnesses and at the same time he would avoid the inevitable accusations that less than the whole amount had been returned. The family concerned were relatives of Debohari's wife and, at least up to that point, they had all been good friends. But everyone lived in perpetual mistrust of everyone else, when money was involved.

They also mistrusted anything to do with government. The post office opened only at regulation hours, not that late at night, and I suppose the intention was that the bearer of the money would present himself, with witnesses, during office hours, and duly make a receipted deposit. Post office receipts showed the time of a transaction (guesswork, according to where the sun was), and a receipt issued at a time when the post office should not have been open might not be valid; this expectation is not unreasonable given villagers' experience of bureaucratic propensities for finding fault. But (my memory is) Jodu did not have banking facilities, so the post office could not have officially been involved. None of this—neither my guesses nor what they did—makes much sense unless one assumes that they had evolved a Byzantine way to deal with the infinity of mistrust they had for each other over money matters. All these monetary transactions, anyway, were entered into Suren's ledger.

The divination on Saturday April 11 got off to a bad start. A patch of ground in front of the sirdar's house had been plastered over to make it smooth and clean. Four brass pots were laid out in a square, and a coconut was balanced on top of each one. Within the square, a pattern was made with green leaves and flowers and rice, moistened with milk. Then Rotona drew a grid pattern with lines of turmeric powder (bright yellow) and a red powder and placed a small mound of rice at each intersection. Then four youths were sat down, lotus fashion, facing inward at each corner of the square. Four clay pots with water from the well were placed on the ground, one beside each youth. Then Rotona blended rice with colored powders, flower petals, and milk and placed a little of this mixture on the head of each boy. All the time he was doing this the Pano musicians were drumming. As he completed the arrangements, the drumming became louder and more insistent, reaching its climax when he stood before the boys and flung handfuls of rice over them, shouting the name of the divinity. He was, I surmised, summoning his devata, whose name I later confirmed was Mauli, to take possession of their bodies.

Nothing happened. Rotona motioned to the drummers, who began to build up another crescendo; more rice was thrown; again he shouted to Mauli. Again nothing happened. The youths grinned at one another, looking slightly embarrassed; at the third and fourth attempts they began to look bored and uncomfortable. They were sitting in the full sun.

There was a short conference, after which Jaya came across to me and asked me to move farther away. "When a lord (*thakur*) stands in front, often a devata will not come." I wondered again if it was not rather the power of my unbelief that they had in mind. I moved way back onto the sirdar's veranda, into the shade. The invocation was repeated; still the boys remained unpossessed. Rotona went into conference with the sirdar. The drums stopped. The boys still sat there in the sun, liquid trickling down their heads, swatting at the flies the moisture attracted. (People in Bisipara swat to move insects along, not to squash them.)

Then the sirdar got to his feet and announced that someone was imprisoning Mauli and making it impossible for her to enter the boys. They would therefore conduct a divination with a charpoy to find out which devata was holding Mauli back. I never found out which was the devata designated to do the detective work, and I suspect that in the end they decided that Mauli, who had not possessed the youths, could nevertheless be persuaded to enter a charpoy. (Nor, unfortunately, did I ask how they would have proceeded if the boys had been possessed by Mauli.)

They set the charpoy up in much the same way as I had seen them do before. It was placed on the cleared ground, the remains of the previous ritual being pushed aside. Bells were fastened to it, and strips of cloth, and a new cloth was laid across the head and another at the foot. A mixture of rice and milk and the colored powders was placed on the ground at each of the four legs. Then Rotona came forward with a chicken and went round each leg in turn, waiting until the bird pecked at the rice. Then he cut off its head and sprayed the blood at the four corners. The youths picked up the cot, each holding one of its legs in his upturned palm. The drummers worked up to a climax, and the charpoy seemed to agitate itself and then settle into a steady slow swinging motion. People evidently interpreted the movement as a sign that the devata had taken possession of the charpoy. Followed immediately by the sirdar, who was to put the questions to it, the cot set off on its search. Rotona stayed behind, sitting on the veranda, crestfallen, looking like an athlete who has just lost a race that he had been billed to win.

I followed Mauli (if that is who it was) some of the way. The charpoy went to the mandap first, then into the sirdar's courtyard, then outside the village to the shrine near Pano street where Thakurani resides; then it came back and spent some time nosing around Tuta's garden, then to the house of Oruno the Brahmin, then to Srimati's house in Hatopodera, and then to a house in Potter street where a devata was known to live. It seemed to me to be moving with a purpose, as if following a well-marked route. I left it then. I heard later that it made a final round of the village streets, the purpose being to imprison whatever devatas were present until a more capable gunia could be brought to clear them out. About two hours had passed since the charpoy was first made ready, and by noon they were all back inside their houses, sheltering from the midday heat.

I watched some of Mauli's investigations, and I could detect nothing different from what had been done on the previous occasion. The sirdar talked to the charpoy in Kui; sometimes it hardly moved; sometimes it swung more vigorously; everywhere it stopped someone threw a handful of rice over it before it departed for the next place. Sometimes they threw water over it to cool it. But, whatever the signs were, I failed to read them. There was a consensus in the village that the divination had been a total failure. Nothing was found; not even all the known resident devatas, Jaya said, were recognized.

I heard a few explanations for failure; not many. The old man living on Warrior street who was the sirdar of a neighboring district was at an age to be interested in sacred things. He was resolutely Hindu in outlook and a bit disdainful of Kond rituals. (He was one of the few who had addressed Bhuani in Oriya.) He asked, scornfully, how Rotona expected his puja to work when he had not even painted his forehead (as a Brahmin would). Jaya, first saying that Rotona must have done something wrong at the beginning, later identified the mistake as a failure to invite Komeswari (the tutelary devata of the Bisois and the village). She, in a dudgeon, had blocked the divination. But later, Jaya said, she had relented and assisted.

Out of this assistance, presumably, came the one positive result. At the end of the divination they put to the charpoy the
names of some well-known gunias, seeking someone whose skills
would be equal to the task. They received a strongly affirmative
answer for a former janitor in the high school in Phulbani, a
man surnamed Patro, who lived in Rotungo. Kopilo told me a
tale about him. In a village called Purapara they had a veritable
plague of devatas. They called in the Patro man, and he made
his puja and sat in front of their mandap and announced that
anywhere a devata was kept it would enter into a woman of that
house and she would come running. Sure enough, in a short
time, three hysterical women came running. The Patro man captured the devatas and thus cleared the village. He was the man
for Bisipara, Kopilo said, and they would soon send a delegation
to invite him. But it was known that Rotungo had a big festival
going at the time, and no one was sure how soon he would be
able to come.

In fact he never did come, and I do not think Bisipara ever sent
a delegation to invite him. Whatever force had been driving the
witch-hunt, now seemed to have died. But there was one final
twitch. Thakurani made a brief appearance.

Thakurani I have glossed as the "smallpox goddess," for she
was firmly associated with that affliction. Her shrine was in the
care of a Pano from the old street, whose name was Hari Behera.
He had taken over the responsibility from his father, four or five
years earlier. A legend attached to that family; they belonged to
a "mark lineage," the mark being the sore that smallpox or a
smallpox vaccination makes on the skin. Before the government
started vaccination for everyone, this family, Jaya said, kept cows
from which they made a serum and administered it to people to
cure their smallpox. (In 1959, living elsewhere in Orissa, I was
several times told by serious men with university degrees that in
the Sanskrit literature all possible knowledge is to be found. If
one knows where to look one can find the design for an aeroplane
or for making an atom bomb.) When the government started its
own program the Behera lineage closed its practice and took em-

ployment as government vaccinators. Hari did not have that job; instead he made a living off the shrine.

When anyone fell sick, especially with an illness that caused a rash, Hari was called. He prescribed what they must give to the devata; sometimes it was only milk, sometimes it was a goat. Then he would blow water on them and go away. If the patient recovered, the promised payment came due the following Tuesday, if it was milk, and, if a goat, at the next annual ceremony that Hari put on for Thakurani. Every Tuesday Hari made a puja at the shrine. (Tuesdays and Fridays are days of ill omen in Bisipara.) He also made the rounds of Kond villages, making Thakurani's services available to the people who lived there. At the annual ceremony the accumulated goats were slaughtered, half of each animal going to the donor and half to the people of Pano street. Thakurani also provided a goat for clean-caste people to arrange a feast in her honor. They held the feast outside the confines of the village; nor did they think it advisable for the meat to be eaten by any man whose wife was pregnant. These provisions indicate that a degree of caution was appropriate in dealing with the smallpox devata.

In 1953 the annual puja for Thakurani was held on April 20 and 21. On the first of these days I was sitting with some men in the shade of the robust pergola-like construction that stands in the middle of Warrior street, east of the mandap. A troop of Pano drummers arrived (all of them from the old street) escorting Hari. Hari had painted his forehead and was weaving about and dancing a few steps and shaking and making all the movements that are appropriate when one is about to be possessed. He sat on the ground, some yards away from us, and almost instantly became possessed by Thakurani; he babbled nonsense and he threw himself about and he rolled his eyes. The performance was not in the least convincing because two of his escorts had got into a violent argument and were not only ignoring his antics but also beginning to attract attention away from him. Hari, clearly exasperated, came out of his trance twice to tell them to shut up. The men around me were watching this scene, evidently amused.

Then Hari shut off the signs of possession and said in a loud clear voice that he had learned from Thakurani that the devata in Tuta's house could be persuaded to go away only if given an offering of human blood. The men around me laughed, and one of them asked where he hoped to get that. I suppose they knew what was coming, but Hari surprised me. He took something from the stuff on the ground in front of him—perhaps a small knife or a sliver of bamboo—and cut his tongue, producing enough blood to smear his lips and drain a little into a bowl. Then he started quivering again and muttering, stood up, danced around for a moment, and then rushed off up the street to Tuta's house, clutching the bowl of blood.

Possessed by Thakurani, Hari was no longer an untouchable but Thakurani herself, and thus exempt from the everyday rule that untouchables do not enter the homes of people of clean caste. He barged inside and found that Tuta was not there. So he began to berate Tuta's wife, urging her that the house should be cleansed of its evil. She was, I heard, not much impressed, her elder son even less so. The son seized an axe and told Hari to do whatever he had to do quickly, and do it properly, otherwise the axe would be used to produce enough of Hari's blood to fill the bowl. After that the work in Tuta's house was quickly done, and soon Hari and the musicians retreated to Pano street. I heard them drumming far into the night and, along with it, an occasional outburst of drunken quarreling. The following day the goats were slaughtered and there was feasting.

That was the last I saw that summer of any public activity that had to do with Susila's death and Tuta's devata.

There is a quite clear pattern in what I detected to be the mood of people around me during the month and two days that elapsed between Susila's death and this last more or less comical episode with Hari Behera and the shedding of his blood. I see myself now as having watched a play in five acts. In the first act, which ran from the time I was taken to see Susila until they were launched into the first divination, the mood was a combination of grief, anxiety, and anger; and none of these emotions seemed contrived. They sank their enmities (between the Warrior factions) and worked as—and seemingly felt themselves to be—an undivided community. There could have been—perhaps there was—a small rift over the time to be spent in mourning for Susila, but it was barely allowed to come out into the open. Normally the factions took pains to probe at small differences until they became big ones; but not this time. During the entire episode, there was no other period when I was so sure that my diagnosis of how people felt was accurate and so confident that the emotions they displayed had in them no element of pretense.

The second act was marked by that curious elation that I described earlier. The initial anxiety quite noticeably gave way to a mood that combined critical interest in the work being done with the enjoyment that comes from theater. People were excited and behaved as if they were about to be in at a kill, although as yet no particular quarry had been publicly identified. They were an audience, anticipating a climax. Of course, as I saw it, they *were* in reality not only watching a performance but also playing their parts in it, acting out an allegory that presented in fantasy their world of experience, the struggles of each one of them with life's uncertainties, and the strivings of their community to maintain its moral integrity against the avarice of individuals. But they did not see it that way at all. For them the divination was not a portrayal of the human condition, but something directly instrumental, an action that would literally modify their environment by removing a malignancy. As they defined the situation, they were watching an operation—in either of the senses (medical or military) of that word.

I deduce the mood of the third act from the haste with which they fixed penalties and the quite trivial sums at which they assessed the offenses. For most people—not, I suppose, Susila's parents—by then the episode was over. The community had diagnosed the source of its sickness and effected a cure. The circle was closed and life was back to normal. The ritual had done what people say rituals do; it had brought about a catharsis. The people also seemed to have done what I had been taught a small community does everywhere: it had subordinated punishment and retribution to the community's need for harmony. Only complex societies, where people do not directly depend on their neighbors to keep life going, can afford the luxury of rigidly enforced, disabling penalties. The Bisipara case was all the more exemplary because the need for harmony was not a vaguely understood desirable state of affairs but something immediate, sharply defined and specific, almost technical: they had to have the screen clear for Ramnobomi.

That third act should have been the last. The story of Susila's death, at least as it emerged in the public domain, could have ended neatly there. But along came a fourth act that exactly reversed the move toward harmony. Now they began to insist on retribution and punishment, in a small way at first (Ramnobomi still filled most of the space available for public action) and then, when the festival was finished, with rapidly increased intensity. It was as if, having papered over the cracks during the third act, they were now determined not only to uncover the cracks but to make them wider and more visible.

In the fourth act the drive to punish gathered momentum when Sadhu's wife was possessed. It came obviously to its climax when Tuta laid sixty rupees at the sirdar's feet. That event, albeit partway through a meeting, ended the fourth act. The fifth and final act was a winding down into—I am sure inadvertent—fiasco; it ended eventually with the comedy put on by Hari. The fires had gone out. Rotona failed, and they talked about his failure, but without urgency, and they made plans to try again. But they never did try again. Whatever (or whoever) had been pushing things along, since the first morning when Sripati brought the news that a conspiracy was in the making, was doing so no longer.

The first three acts—collective anxiety as Susila lay dying, the divination, and the swift settlement—were produced and directed by the community. The community's primary value— health and safety ensured by morally correct conduct and communal harmony—was placed center stage. Parties normally unwilling to cooperate sank their differences and worked together; and when they found out who had offended, they acted quickly and mostly without vindictiveness to bring them back into the fold. But the fourth act was put on by a different management.

The day after Hari Behera's sideshow, Tuta's son, the one who had intimidated Hari, came to the bungalow to ask for medicine. I stuck a thermometer under his arm, a ritual gesture since the back of his neck was burning hot and I could see he was shivering despite the noonday heat. (I had early learned that thermometers in the mouth made people in Bisipara very uneasy.) While we waited for the thermometer to register, I asked him about Hari's visit. The question opened a gate. The sirdar, the young man said, had put "the Harijan" up to it. His father stood alone, and what could he do against all the village? He repeated this several times. Then I remembered that Kopilo had mentioned some earlier quarrel between the sirdar and the two Washermen brothers, when they had fled from Bisipara. I asked about it. The trouble started, the young man said, when his father's mother died. The Bisipara Brahmin (Oruno's father) refused to make the puja they requested. So they paid ten rupees to a Brahmin from Phiringia to come and officiate. The sirdar then turned on them and drove them from the village. His father stayed away several years and came back only when Bisipara people invited him, because they could not find another Washerman to do the work.

The story, plausible in its main features, invited further questioning. But that did not seem appropriate at the time, and I handed over Paludrine tablets and watched him swallow the first dose. I intended to follow up the several leads another time. But I never did. It was not so much the literal historical truth that I wanted, as what the people perceived to be a reasonable justification for the actions said to have been taken. If Oruno's father did turn them down, why did he do it? What would have been advanced as a good reason? Washermen are very low in the caste hierarchy, and Oruno's father may have been less liberal than the Brahmin who was hired. Or it could have been something personal, something not a matter of principle at all. Why did the sirdar intervene? Again it could have been a personal vendetta. Or the sirdar might have felt that the proper order of things— the ritual standing of different castes and therefore the community's moral integrity, its dharma—was being put in danger by Washermen getting above themselves and paying money to bring in a blackleg Brahmin. Perhaps, even that recently, it was felt that Washermen had no right to the services of a Brahmin at their family rituals. I do not know the answers.

The next day (April 22) a Distiller, Ramo Pradhan, came to the bungalow, asking me to go to his house. His wife had been taken ill; she had a fever and diarrhea—I guessed bacillary dysentery. I gave her the one medicine I had for that affliction, sulfaguanidine, which requires the patient to swallow a very large number of tablets at one time. I waited there while she took the first dose, knowing that sometimes people liked to try out one or two tablets and see if that would work, and so be able to keep the rest for the next illness. (Fortunately she got better.)

Ramo and I sat outside his house on the veranda and I asked him what he made of Hari Behera's possession. I was graduating from the thought that at first always came to me unbidden— surely none of them really believed in devatas. The new thought was that surely at least some of them did not believe in devatas. This time I think I had what I wanted. Ramo asked, rhetorically, if we had devatas that ate people in England, and, not waiting for an answer, gestured toward Warrior street and said, "It's the Bisois. They do it. It's the sirdar."

When I wrote the note on that conversation I surely thought that I had found a second skeptical person to go along with the (possibly) skeptical carpenter, who at the outset had insisted that Susila was suffering from a sickness, not a devata. The rhetorical question about the prevalence of devatas in England is, I think, evidence that Ramo did not believe in devatas, or at least that he was ready to assert when talking to me that he did not. Once again I can conceive now of further conversation that might have made the matter less uncertain. For example I could have asked him why, if there were no devatas, did Susila die. But I did not.

Providing I have made the right deduction from his rhetorical question Ramo remains the one unambiguously unbelieving person in Bisipara in the matter of devatas. All my other fishing for skepticism caught nothing. Debohari's and Jaya's statements that devatas cannot harm those who do not believe in them testify to the limited power of devatas; their existence is not put in doubt. When people were skeptical about particular performances—Bhuani's inability to find the coin I had hidden or Rotona's total failure—they were questioning the technical abilities of the experts, not the correctness of the science itself. When Tuta's son blamed the sirdar for manipulating Hari Behera, he too was not questioning the system; he was explaining how the system had been exploited so as to victimize his father.

Given this generalized belief, my sense is that the problem would have been solved for them and the entire affair would have come to an end with act three (the Bhuani divination and the payment of modest fines), if the sirdar and his cronies had not worked to keep the issue warm until Ramnobomi ended, and then, helped out by the presumably genuine seizure of Sadhu's wife, heated up the pot until it boiled. Tuta's sixty rupees then cooled everything down, and the sirdar, having got what he wanted, let matters drift into nothingness, as they usually do if no one takes the trouble to push them along and guide them.

Seen from that perspective, several things fall into place. In their hearts, one may surmise, everyone knew that the matter was really concluded on March 21, when Bhuani had done her work and the fines had been paid. The communal sense of urgency had been dissipated. But it was soon replaced, as the driving force, by the manipulative skills and energies of a few people who stood to gain by intensifying the witch-hunt. Between the fines and the levy of one rupee from each house far more money was collected after April 6 than was needed for, or was expended on, cleansing ceremonies. Once Tuta's savings had been garnisheed, only small sums were spent on Rotona's performance, and the potentially more expensive Patro expert was never brought on the scene.

The community saved its money. The community benefited; so did Sri Ramchandro; so, perhaps, did the sirdar.

Have I then found, in the person of the sirdar, a Bisipara version of economic man, the opportunistic individual motivated only by his own advantage, ever ready to use public concerns for private gain? In the journal of public events that Debohari kept for me in 1954 when I was away and continued after I came back in 1955, frequent panchayat meetings are recorded in which there are acrimonious disputes about building Sri Ramchandro's new temple. Some of these are about people who did not turn up for communal work when the panchayat demanded it. Some record levies and various other ways of getting money into the fund. More than a few of them are of the kind I mentioned earlier, either veiled or sometimes direct accusations that the sirdar was raiding the fund. I do not know whether he really did so. I do know that people in Bisipara assumed that, where cash is involved, every normal person yields to temptation.

They were wonderfully ambivalent about the sirdar. Several years later, when the unsinkable Basu Pradhan was standing for the chairmanship of the newly established local government council, they tried to have the sirdar nominated, but then discovered that his office made him ineligible. Perhaps they were only working on the principle of "the devil you know," but I suspect their attitude was more complicated than that. Earlier, in one of the altercations in 1954 about missing temple funds, the sirdar volunteered to take an oath before Sri Ramchandro, swearing to his own innocence. But, so the scribe (Debohari) records, people were anxious that he should *not* do so, for if he were lying, he would come to great harm. Exactly the same sequence of events occurred in 1955, when the sirdar and another man, his partner in a contract, accused each other of stealing money allocated to buy tiles for the new temple. Each offered to take an oath and actually presented himself at the temple, properly bathed and with the appropriate offerings. But an impassioned speech from Susila's father about the dangers involved persuaded the villagers to prevent the ceremony from going forward. To think that way, they must have suspected that the sirdar was lying and he had helped himself to Sri Ramchandro's cash. They must also have valued the sirdar. But whether they did so intrinsically, seeing in him a symbol of a social order that was morally beyond question (but was now under threat), or whether they were grateful for the small protections he could sometimes provide from the intrusions of government agents, is hard to tell. (Romesh said that both men were lying, both had pocketed some of the money, and had then conspired together to confuse the issue by accusing each other.)

There was ambiguity and ambivalence on every side. By 1953, for about a century an alien and very authoritarian bureaucracy had exposed Bisipara to the winds of change. It did not do so deliberately. Government in the Kond hills, as in many parts of India before 1947, was kept at a low level, because higher levels would be expensive. Low levels of government mostly mean keeping things as they are; conservatism is cheap (at least in the short run), radical change may be costly. The administration tried to let things be as they imagined things always had been. But in fact, by pacifying the region and building a few roads and opening a few markets, they turned the world of the ordinary villagers upside down. They did not intend to do so. Administrators tried to work through traditional collectivities, through existing communities, the Kond muthas and the villages. But the effect of better communications and of *pax brittanica* was to undermine the authority of traditional communities and open the way to individual entrepreneurs. But the way was not wide open. Government courts focused on individuals and their rights; but the bureaucracy, when making rules and setting policies, generally treated individuals as inseparable from the collectivities in which they lived—villages, or castes, or ethnic groupings. There was a heated debate in the Constituent Assembly, which met in Delhi between 1947 and 1949, about whether India should have a constitution, as Gandhi wished, founded on corporate village communities, or whether India should have a modern constitution based on the rights of the individual citizen. The "individualists" won, but the bureaucracy continued—as is inevitable—to work through categories (such as Harijan or Adibasi) and through collective units, villages, development blocks, and, later, political parties and other formal organizations.

In places like Bisipara, in the backwoods, where before 1947 (and to some extent still afterward) the rulers and the ruled were different people, it was as if a single thread linked government to villagers. The thread was *imperium*, overlordship, a relationship of power (even if sometimes contested) and nothing else. Villagers dealt with each other in many different ways, as they made their living, as they followed their religion, as they were kin or neighbors to one another, and as they competed over the distribution of power. It was this very complexity, this interweaving of different activities, that made them a community, that rounded out relationships, and at the same time gave rise to moral feelings and a sense of duty. The single thread of imperium between villagers and government, at least in 1953, carried no essential morality. It was a matter of instrumentality, where each person used the other for his own advantage.

The villagers themselves were moving in that direction in their dealings with one another. Those halfway into the other world, like Basu Pradhan, were used by the villagers, when that was possible, but never trusted. Cash and the market provided the solvent that was breaking down community values. In 1953 the people of Bisipara were thoroughly ambivalent between duty to the collectivity and the right of individuals to do what was best for themselves. Matters that were unconnected with cash they could regulate without much difficulty. No one planted a paddy field until the sirdar's household had ceremonially opened the season with the appropriate ritual. Harvesting various crops also waited on the collective decision about "first fruit" ceremonies. They had trouble, however, regulating the wages of day laborers, endeavoring to hold them down in the planting season, when labor was scarce. Farm laborers were no longer family retainers, but entrepreneurs selling their labor on a market. Other economic activities, those that belonged unambiguously in the domain of commerce and the market, they did not try to regulate, and they assumed, like any orthodox neoclassical economist, that self-interest would always prevail. A small irrigation dam that the government built north of the village collapsed in 1951. It collapsed, they explained to me, because it was put up by a contractor and the contractor had cheated. But the high-piered bridge across the Salki a mile south of the village, built back in the 1930s by their own forced labor (*bheti*) under the direction of government engineers, was a fine and solid construction, of which they spoke with pride.

Indeed, they seemed to believe that the very token of the new economy—cash—would be sufficient in itself to make a person dishonest and careless of his or her public responsibilities. Cash had no place in the image that Bisipara people used to talk about their distant past and to portray the truly moral life, the life that was right and proper, in accordance with the divine intention, and therefore safe and secure. Morality belonged in the world that I described earlier, turning around a central brotherhood of Warrior males, who were like a star around which orbited both their women and the castes dependent on them. It was an ordered hierarchical world, founded on inherited wealth that came from the land and guarded by divine beings whose goodwill must be sought by gifts and deference, just as in life those who hold power must be propitiated and honored by lesser people who depend upon them. When things go wrong, when crops fail or the rains do not come, or people die before their time, the reason always is that the divinely ordained order, the moral order, has been violated. In a sense all failure is ultimately caused by individual failings, individual wickedness.

This, of course, was not the only image they had; they were aware of other possibilities, for example the curiously unreal moral world (unreal as they saw it) portrayed in the Gandhian ideal of a society without untouchability. (Letters at that time were franked, in English, with the sentence "Untouchability has been abolished.") They were also aware of their present reality in which erstwhile dependents, such as the Panos, protested the system in the name of democracy. Even in 1953 they were hearing electoral rhetoric claiming that their political masters were the servants of the people, and they took the message with a large grain of salt, because the hierarchy they knew did not work that way; nor did they think it should.

They also had an image of reality that, change and innovation aside, recognized the essential contradictions of social life, the inevitable conflict of interest between the contained and the container. We tend to focus on the two extremes: individual rights (the contained) set against the demands of society (the container). But an exactly similar opposition goes on all the way upward and outward: first individual, then man and wife, then man and wife and children, them against the joint family, families within a faction, factions within a caste, castes within a village or across the countryside, villagers against townsmen and officials, and so on; and there are other more general oppositions, such as old against young, male against female, even, in Bisipara, the community against malevolent devatas.

All these conflicts, whether perennial or recognized as the outcome of changes in the recent past, had to be moderated. The image in Bisipara of the distant past, of the truly moral life, was not a reality to be presently enjoyed but a vision toward which everyone must strive. The vision was essentially a conservative one: stay in place, keep things in place. But things were not in place. There were Panos, a few, who owned nearly as much land as the richest Warrior. Others were men of influence, such as Sindhu the schoolmaster or two men who were active in electoral politics at the district and state level. The Distillers, once a humble clean caste, were now major landowners and, head for head, in no way economically inferior to the Warriors. Moreover the control that once had made it possible for Warriors to dominate—the use of force—had been yielded to the government. Government courts, any time the officials wished, could set aside decisions by the Warrior-dominated panchayat.

Against the background of this topsy-turvy world the events of

March and April reveal their full complexity. The sirdar's vendetta was surely self-interested. But it could also have been altruistic. He may not have been embezzling the money to pay off his debts to government; he may have been driven by the vow he had made to build a new temple for Sri Ramchandro. That would add to his spiritual merit, but it would also bring blessings (and ordinary everyday kudos) for the village. Tuta was the victim of the sirdar's manipulations, because Tuta was rich enough to be worth plucking and was a marginal person, low in the caste hierarchy, and, as his son said, he stood alone. On the other hand he was a Washerman who had risen to a level of prosperity above that appropriate to his status. Therefore to bring him down was to do something good for the moral order.

In the end I can say nothing that I know for sure to be historically accurate about motivations. I do know what Bisipara's cultural deck of cards looked like. I also had some knowledge of how hands could conventionally be played, and I could attach hypothetical outcomes to each strategy. But I could never have forecast how they actually were played, still less how each game would turn out.

Now that you have read this story, you may wish to know where the truth lies. But there is not much uncontestable truth; mostly there are choices. Here they are.

The sirdar, representing the ordinary man, would say that Tuta kept a devata that ran amok and killed Susila and the Herdsman child, and Tuta paid a sixty-rupee penalty. I suppose many people in Bisipara believed that. You, since you are reading this book in English, probably do not.

The sirdar also might say that Tuta, besides being a wicked man who behaved irresponsibly by keeping a devata, also was someone heading for a fall. He had gotten much richer than was right for a Washerman, and had done so by the unethical use of Durga, and therefore had to be brought back into line. Bringing him back into line restored the moral balance that his wickedness had disturbed. You, the reader, may not accept the moral judgment, but at least you understand that, if the sirdar was motivated in that way, he only followed his conscience in what he did. (Whether he was also able to help himself, personally, by doing the right thing, could be beside the point.)

The obverse of this interpretation, also shared by people in Bisipara, was that the sirdar was short of money to pay his debts to the government (or to mend his bicycle) and was not scrupulous about how he got it. Tuta got into trouble mainly because he had enough money to pay a large fine and did not have enough friends to protect him. If he had invested money in patron-client ties, as Basu Pradhan had, he would not have been a victim. But probably he did not have enough wealth to do that. The best course available to him was to pay protection money—the sixty rupees—to the village boss. Whether the boss in question was Sri Ramchandro or the sirdar remains uncertain.

The detached outsider also has choices, some of which parallel the various Bisipara opinions. Whatever his motivations, the *consequence* of the sirdar's maneuvering was the reaffirmation of the fundamental values of the society. Thus, in a curious way, even if the sirdar's actions were selfishly motivated, their result was the public good (that is, the orthodox version of it). Morality triumphed. A noneconomic manifestation of Adam Smith's invisible hand was at work. The Washerman and people of all the other specialist castes were reminded that God had ordained a place for them in society, and their well-being could be assured only by staying in that place. A Washerman who evolved into a prosperous capitalist was an evolutionary quirk, unfit for survival. The irony of this verdict, of course, is that the Washerman's downfall may have happened only because the sirdar himself was likewise eager to make money.

Tuta, the entrepreneur, leasing land, lending money, lending paddy, and trading in the market, represented a new order, which the conservative mind saw as a new disorder. But the new disorder might in fact not be that at all. It could be Adam Smith's economic way: an entrepreneur creating new wealth that might indeed alter the pattern of society but would in the end allow everyone to have a share in a new and better way of life. From that point of view the tragedy in this episode was that Tuta, the entrepreneur, succumbed to the forces of reaction. His story epitomizes, perhaps, the nightmare of all the liberal-inclined free-enterprise-touting planners and developers that the United States sprinkled around the Third World from the 1950s onward.

If there is truth, it is some combination of all these choices. The story of Tuta's tribulation unfolds not only as a community fighting back against selfish individualism, but also (somewhat inflating Tuta's stature) as an individual heroically failing in his struggle to make his own way in life. It is also the story of a rational individual (the sirdar) exploiting community values in order to line his own pocket. But I do not know the truth about motives. Perhaps—the unresolvable question—the sirdar did what he did in order to protect a way of life, the dharma in which he and others sincerely believed. But even if he was not motivated to protect that dharma, the consequences of what he did had exactly that effect: Tuta was brought back into line, and Bisipara's hierarchy was restored and reinforced. For those as cynical as myself and Ramo the Distiller, the witch-hunt made one thing very clear: it paid (both the victims and the victimizers) to behave as if they believed in the customary moral order.

In principle I should have been able to find out the truth about events (as distinct from motivations), but, as has been obvious, I am not at all sure about the details of what really went on in Bisipara in 1953. Did Sripati invent the story about the plot to appeal to the courts? Was he told by the sirdar to invent it? I do not know what the three accused men said when confronted with the tale. I do not even know if they were confronted in any formal way. What I am confident about is the structural reality that allowed me to make sense of what I saw going on: the central corporate core of male Bisois, the threat to their solidarity posed by the women they had to bring in from outside, the threat to their power posed by specialist castes, and, an altogether more serious danger for the existing hierarchy, the slowly intensifying revolutionary discontinuities introduced after the Meriah Wars by an alien administration. This context, together with the ubiquitous and self-contradictory human ambition to enjoy a secure life among people who, you believe, make your life insecure because they are driven by self-interest, generated the witch-hunt in Bisipara in 1953.

At the end of October 1953 Tuta made a verbal petition to the panchayat. He said that Syamo Bisoi (Susila's father), the old women in the Herdsman house next to his (Rua and the grandmother of the dead child), and several other people whom he named (including Romesh) were going about saying his daughters were handmaidens of a devata. Tuta said he had paid over money as punishment for whatever fault there was, and they had no right to say such things. The panchayat agreed and ordered there should be no more such talk. (I am sure there was. Jaya's scathing text on sorcery and Tuta as a sorcerer was written well after that time.)

A meeting in early January 1954 decided that each household should cut its harvesttime jajmani payment of paddy to the Washerman by one quarter, since he had done no jajmani work for them over a period of three months in the preceding year.

I have a final note on Tuta and the sirdar. It is part of the journal kept by Debohari and it is dated February 7, 1954.

> The sirdar summoned a meeting of the panchayat to discuss a complaint that the dhoba was washing clothes only for [there follows a list of households in the sirdar's faction]. The dhoba said, "This is what I want to do. There is no reason to get angry about it." Thereupon Madhia [in Jodu the postmaster's faction] said, "They give you rice. What do we give you? Dirt?" When the dhoba said what he intended to do, [Jodu's party] decided that they would find another dhoba.

The sirdar and his faction, throughout the time I kept in touch with events in Bisipara, were always the stronger. They were, at that time, the final arbiters of Bisipara's moral order.

Glossary

Words marked (K) are Kui. The rest are Oriya.

anto: an unleveled field
baidyo: a doctor
bara sahib: an important person
berna: an irrigated field area
bhato: cooked rice
bheti: forced labor
bhumi: the earth
bhuto: the ghost of a person who died in unfortunate circumstances
bidi: a country style of cigarette
bilati baigono: tomato
bonobasi: dweller in the jungle (the third stage of Hindu life)
brata: an amulet
caulo: husked rice
dahinga (K): slash-and-burn fields
dali: dal; pulses; lentils
dehuri: a priest
devata: a divinity
dhano: paddy
dharma: custom; way of life; duty; the natural order of things
dhoba: washerman
dhoti: a man's garment
doladoli: faction fighting
dolo: faction; party
ga loko samaste: all the people of the village
gamucha: a towel or shawl

ghi: clarified butter

golmal: altercation

gunia: a diviner; a ritual specialist

jajman: a landholder employing servants

jajmani: the relationship of a *jajman* and a *kamin*

jati puo: a man of the same caste, related through women

jatra: a festival

kacha: rough; unfinished; coarse

kamin: a servant employed by a *jajman*

kendu: a kind of shrub (*Dyospyros menalexylon*)

khetu: a leveled irrigated field

khorap: rotten

khushi re: in happiness

kondho: Kond

lia: paddy kernels popped by heating

lungi: a man's garment

mahua: a kind of tree (*Bassia latifolia*)

maitro: a ritual friend

mamughoro: the maternal uncle's house

mamul: dues owed to a feudal superior

mandap: a meeting house

meriah: a form of human sacrifice; the victim of such a sacrifice

modu: liquor prepared from *mahua* flowers

mohuri: an oboe

mrudungo: a type of drum

mudi: rice kernels popped by heating

mutha: an administrative area

namaskar: a form of greeting; a gesture of respect, palms together

nangeli pota (K): the plough bird

orua caulo: rice husked from unboiled paddy

pakka: finished; proper; refined

pan: a plug for chewing prepared from betel leaves and areca-nut parings and various spices

panchayat: a council

penu (K): a divinity

pidera: ancestral spirits

puja: a Hindu rite of worship

raj: the government

raja-praja: king-subject; a feudal relationship

rokhiba: to keep

sag: wild spinach

sahukar: a shopkeeper, merchant; a store

sal: a kind of tree (*Shorea robusta*)

samaj: an association

sari: a woman's garment; also a turban bestowed on an officeholder

sirdar: a person in charge of a *mutha*

sito: purified

soru (K): the mountain (paired with *tana,* the earth)

sraddha: a funeral rite

tambi: a measure of volume, approximately a quart

tana (K): the earth (paired with *soru,* the mountain)

thakur: a lord

torkari: a curry, usually of vegetables

usna caulo: rice husked from boiled paddy

Index